IRISH COMIC POEMS

IRISH COMIC POEMS

Selected and translated by

CRIOSTOIR O'FLYNN

Cló Iar-Chonnachta
Indreabhán
Conamara

An Chéad Chló 1995

ISBN 1 874700 33 8

Pictiúr Clúdaigh
Pádraig Reaney

Dearadh Clúdaigh
Johan Hofteenge

Dearadh
Foireann CIC

Faigheann Cló Iar-Chonnachta Teo., cabhair airgid ón **gComhairle Ealaíon.**

Clóchur: Cló Iar-Chonnachta Teo., Indreabhán, Conamara.
Fón: 091-93307
Priontáil: Clódóirí Lurgan Teo., Indreabhán, Conamara.
Fón: 091-93251/93157

For Liam and Jake in whose company this book was started

Buíochas le lucht cóipchirt as cead na dánta thíos a athfhoilsiú:

Sáirséal Ó Márcaigh; *Tulyar* le Seán Ó Ríordáin
An Clóchomhar; *Faoileán Drochmhúinte* le Máirtín Ó Direáin

CONTENTS

1. Oisín's Lament in Old Age – *Anonymous* 26
2. The Dialogue of Pádraig and Oisín – *Anonymous* 29
3. Dying of Love – *Anonymous* 41
4. The Monk's Welcome to the Herring – *Anonymous* 47
5. The Woman of Three Cows – *Anonymous* 53
6. On Miley's Tombstone – *Anonymous* 59
7. To a Snorer – *Anonymous* 63
8. The Yellow Bittern – *Cathal Buí Mac Giolla Gunna* (16?? – 1750) 69
9. The Brandy – *Diarmuid Ó Súilleabháin* (1680 – 1750) 75
10. Cock-eyed Mary – *Art Mac Cubhtaigh* (1715 – 1773) 80
11. They're Best Left Alone – *Eoghan Rua Ó Súilleabháin* (1748 – 1784) 86
12. Protestant or Papist – *Áindréas Mac Craith* (1710 – 1795)........ 95
13. The Merry Publican – *Seán Ó Tuama* (1708 – 1775) 101
14. Response of an Angry Customer – *Aindréas Mac Craith* (1710 – 1795) 105
15. The Adventure of Misfortune's Minion – *Donncha Rua Mac Conmara* (1715 – 1810) 111

16. Wedded Bliss: two extracts from
The Midnight Court –
Brian Merriman (17?? – 1805) 134
17. Lament for a Bailiff – *Riocard Bairéad*
(1739 – 1819) 150
18. Blind Raftery and the Thorn Tree –
Antoine Ó Reachtabhra (1784 – 1835) ... 155
19. A Malediction on Tobacco –
Anonymous 166
20. The New Maestro – *Art Beanaid*
(1820 – 1860) 170
21. The Spinning Wheel – *Anonymous* 174
22. The Little White Horse –
Seoirse Seártan (1875 – 1924) 178
23. Tulyar – *Seán Ó Ríordáin* (1918 – 1977) 184
24. To an Uncouth Seagull –
Máirtín Ó Direáin (1910 – 1988) 188

Introduction

When I began to search through the books on my shelves and in the National Library to find the raw material for this collection, I was pulled up sharp, given pause as the saying is, by a scholarly but pedantic commentator. As I thumbed once more through *Meascra Dánta*, an anthology of mostly medieval poems edited by Professor Tomás Ó Rathaille in 1927, I came across a short comic piece which I had always enjoyed. But in the notes to that book, the learned editor's comment on this quaint little poem is academically snooty: "My excuse for including this rather trifling piece, " says he, "is the paucity of light or humorous poems in our MSS." That could have put a spanner in my poetic works if I had not learned long ago that the creative writer and the scholarly academic are birds of a very different feather. So, reading the poem once again, I still judged it to be a well-made poem that tickled my fancy and might have the same effect on others; judge for yourself, dear reader – it is included in this collection under the title *On Miley's Tombstone*.

However, with the second part of the Professor/Editor's comment I totally agree. Truly comic poems are very few and far between in what has survived of Irish literature from previous centuries. It may be a truism, but it needs to be repeated in this present context: the Irish people and their poets had very little to wax comic about for the past seven hundred years. And in modern times, like poets everywhere in this century of World Wars, atomic weapons and global pollution, poets in Ireland seem to be wallowing in Bunyan's "Slough of Despond" or else they find their material in narcissistic personal trivia or in free-verse effusions which are often inscribed to some fellow-poet for some reason not apparent to the mystified reader.

One of my favourite authors, G.K. Chesterton, was a genius who, like his equally robust and rotund predecessor, Dr. Samuel Johnson, had to earn his daily crust by literary hack-work. Consequently, he could craft a real poem like *The Donkey* one day and on another churn out jingoistic or pietistic doggerel. It must have been on one of his hacking days that he delivered himself of the following:

"The great Gaels of Ireland
Are the men that God made mad
For all their wars are merry
And all their songs are sad."

Obviously, the ebullient G.K.C. never found himself between two warring Irish clans – and one wonders what he would make of the recent quarter century of sectarian savagery that is part of the bitter heritage of imperialism in this island and that has left over three thousand corpses strewn across six of the nine counties of Ulster and extended its indiscriminate slaughtering even to the streets of London and other cities in Britain. But Chesterton seems to have sat in some Irish pubs, for just as one can readily agree with Professor Ó Rathaille as to the "paucity of light or humorous poems in our MSS," one can also agree, more or less, with the convivial G.K.C. when he judged that the songs of the Irish are generally sad. After a few pints, any group of Irishmen in a pub will entertain or bore the company with an endless fund of funny stories, even the more bawdy of which often have a core of genuine wit; but as soon as they arrive at the singing stage – if singing is allowed by mine host of the inn – you'll get *Danny Boy, Kathleen Mavourneen, The Old Bog Road, Mother Machree*, etc. And these are only the songs of the anglicised Irish soul. In the ancestral language, the songs are generally political or religious, laments for dead or faithless lovers, or songs of exile, many of them very moving and lyrically beautiful but of little use to the compiler of an anthology of comic poems.

When in 1904 the Gaelic League campaigned for the inclusion of Irish in the curriculum for post-primary and university education, its president, Dr. Douglas Hyde, (one of those who founded the League in 1893 with the idealistic aim of restoring Irish as the spoken language of the people) engaged in a famous dispute with Dr. John Pentland Mahaffy of Trinity College, Dublin, before the Commission appointed to consider the matter. Dr. Mahaffy, then Professor of Ancient History at Trinity and later to become one of its most colourful provosts, bluntly informed the Commission that Irish was practically a dead language, which might conceivably "be of some use to a man when speaking to his gillie in the West of Ireland," and that there was "nothing in Irish literature which was not silly, religious or indecent." Hyde gleefully countered this academic nonsense by pointing out that Mahaffy, who prided himself on his knowledge of classical languages and some continental tongues, and even (until 1914, that is) on his personal acquaintance with the Kaiser, was totally ignorant of Irish and was merely using ammunition supplied by other parties, to oppose which Hyde himself produced the learned opinions of many continental scholars of the Celtic Languages including Irish. But while even today one can wonder at the antagonistic pontifications of an academic like Mahaffy on a topic about which he was personally ignorant, in my search for comic poems in Irish I wondered whether even his inimical declaration that there were many "silly" poems in our literature might not give me some hope of finding suitable material.

Eventually, and obviously, I found sufficient material to make this anthology. But it will be noted by the percipient reader that the Irish sense of humour, as exemplified in many of these poems, is not of the "funny ha-ha" type (although the older prose literature does contain many highly imaginative farcical passages). And in this context I quote from the introduction to another anthology by our learned friend, Professor Tomás Ó Rathaille. His collection of medieval Irish love poetry, *Dánta Grá* (1925), is graced with an interesting preface by the Oxford professor and hibernophile, Dr. Robin Flower, who, unlike Mahaffy of Trinity, did know Irish and was the translator of *An tOileánach* (The Islandman), the autobiography of Blasket Islander, Tomás Ó Criomhthain. Inter alia, Robin Flower says: "There has always been in the Irish nature a sharp and astringent irony, a tendency to react against sentiment and mysticism, an occasional bias to regard life under a clear and humorous light . . . From Mac Conglinne to Merriman the light of this inexhaustible irony plays upon Irish life and letters. We miss the point of much in the literature if we forget this."

We also miss the point if we do not advert to the fact that while the Irish poets and people had little to laugh about, they had plenty of material for satire in all its forms. The poets had to be wary of offending the authorities with their political poems, or the local landlords and their bailiffs with personal lampoons; but they found artistic ways and means of expressing their own and their people's feelings. In political poems, Ireland is given allegorical names like "Róisín Dubh" (*Dark Rosaleen*, as Mangan rendered it) or the macaronic form was used to provide a double-take which must have caused the English soldiers in many a tavern to be agreeably surprised at the conviviality and apparent goodwill of the Irish drinkers.

Donncha Rua Mac Conmara, author of the longest poem in this collection, *The Adventure of Misfortune's Minion*, wrote one of the best-known of these double-meaning poems, a Jacobite song which is still sung and which I would have included in this book but for the obvious fact that the whole point of a macaronic poem is that it must not be "translated." I give the first verse as a matter of interest, with an English version under the Irish lines which would have been sung with such gusto by the "friendly" Irish natives in the taverns of those garrison towns of the eighteenth century:

"As I was walking one evening fair
Is mé go déanach i mBaile Sheáin
(*And I lately in Johnstown*)

I met a gang of English blades
Is iad dá dtraochadh ag a námhaid;
(*And they being destroyed by their enemy*)

I sang and drank so brisk and airy
With those courageous men of war –
'S gur bhinne liom Sasanaigh ag rith le foiréigean
'S gurbh iad clanna Gael bocht a bhuaigh an lá!
(*Sweeter to me the English being forced to run*
And the poor Irish race to have won the day!)

A typical example of the double-take comic satire on a landlord's bailiff is the poem by Riocard Bairéad of County Mayo which is included in this collection.

The Irish sense of humour is also often self-deprecatory in its irony, and I doubt if any other literature can show a better example of this kind of comic poem than the piece in this collection in which a monk welcomes the single herring which stares at him from his monastic dinner-plate on Ash Wednesday.

The kinds and theories of translations of poetry have been a matter of argument and discussion among poets and critics since the abandonment of the Tower of Babel. I am of the Dr. Johnson school: the Sage informed Boswell not only that poetry cannot be defined but that it cannot be translated, and it is thus the highest form of language. Anyone who reads Irish and English with equal ease will not need to be told that my versions of the Irish poems in this book are just that, versions which I hope read well enough to give the reader a vicarious enjoyment of the original as well as some idea of its poetic merit and the skill of its author.

I have endeavoured to keep as closely as possible to the structure of the Irish poems (my English versions of Irish song-poems can hopefully be sung to the same air) but Irish prosody presents the translator with two problems: the older poetry of the bards was syllabic, the most common form being a four-line stanza in which each line contained seven syllables. I have not tried to imitate this, but to give a more or less equivalent value to the line in English. From the seventeenth century onwards, the poets tended to abandon those difficult syllabic metres and to write in the common European stress metre; but they still retained an amazingly complex system of rhyme and of internal assonance which is impossible to match in English.

The prolific use of poetic licence supplied the poets with a store of rhymes beyond the ordinary use of the language, but even a reader who knows nothing of Irish must admire the skill with which Donncha Rua Mac Conmara composed the longest poem in this book, all 286 lines of which end with some form or other of the long "ay" sound followed by a weak syllable. It is of interest to note that Dante in his *Divina Commedia* uses the same kind of ending in his basic eleven-syllable line; but the *terza rima*, or three-line stanza rhyming aba, bcb, cdc, etc., while causing its own technical problems, allows Dante far more variety and freedom to change than the Irish poet, Mac Conmara, gives himself; and yet his rollicking poem flows effortlessly from start to finish, so much so, indeed, that poems like this were memorized and recited by the unschooled and so-called illiterate peasants of that "Hidden Ireland" of the eighteenth century.

Two of the poems in this collection are of special interest to anyone who is curious as to the origin of the metrical form known in English as the "limerick," a form now used principally for bawdy and even obscene compositions by half-wits (I use the term in the Augustan sense). If there existed in English prosody some metrical forms known as the "manchester" or the "liverpool," one would expect that the academic commentators' first deduction would be that these must have some connection with the cities of Manchester or Liverpool respectively. Yet this form known as the "limerick" seems to leave them floundering in stygian ignorance. The Oxford Companion to English Literature has the following:

"*Limerick*, a form of facetious jingle, of which the first instances occur in *Anecdotes and Adventures of Fifteen Young Ladies* and the *History of Sixteen Wonderful Old Women* (1820), subsequently popularized by Edward Lear (q.v.) in his *Book of Nonsense*. (The name is said to be derived from a custom at convivial parties, according to which each member sang an extemporized 'nonsense-verse,' which was followed by a chorus containing the words 'Will you come up to Limerick?' [OED])."

The *Encyclopaedia Britannica*, having devoted two articles to the city and county of Limerick respectively, even giving the original Irish name, *Luimneach*, continues with an entry on the metrical form, the limerick, in which some authority on such matters says:

"The origin of this popular type of nonsense verse is unknown. Langford Reed, the Limerick's only historian and principal anthologist suggested

(*The Complete Limerick Book 1925*) that the name derives from a song brought back from France by returning members of the Irish Brigade in the 18th Century, the chorus of which was *Will you come up to Limerick*? The first collections of Limericks in English date from about 1820."

Both of these prestigious works of reference at least sing the same song, *Will you come up to Limerick*? even if one ascribes it to "a custom at convivial parties" and the other to "returning members of the Irish Brigade in the 18th Century" (where they were returning to we are not told, where they set out from is a matter known to every schoolchild in Ireland – the Irish regiments in the armies of King Louis of France were formed from those soldiers known as the "Wild Geese" who left Ireland after the Treaty of Limerick ended the Williamite wars in 1691, and who, when they heard of the blatant violation of the terms of that Treaty 'before the ink wherewith 'twas writ was dry' adopted as their battle-cry '*Cuimhníg' ar Luimneach is ar fheall na Sasanach*!' – 'Remember Limerick and the treachery of the English!') A point of interest also is the fact that those troops, and their many successors as recruits to the Irish Brigade in France, spoke Irish, not English. It is understandable that those unfortunates, who were mere cannon-fodder in the continental wars between *Le Roi Soleil* and his sworn enemy, William of Orange, and his allies, should feel like singing songs in their native tongue if they succeeded, as very few of them did, in ever returning to Ireland. Why any of them should return to anywhere singing a song in English (especially about Limerick!) must remain a linguistic and cultural mystery.

Even Sherlock Holmes's plodding friend, the elementary Dr. Watson, would have headed straight for the city and county of Limerick. There he would, eventually, have learned of the Irish poets who held a poetic court in the village of Croom in County Limerick in the 18th Century, and of similar poetic gatherings in the city of Limerick and in other parts of Munster. Some of the poems written by members of the County Limerick poetic circle are in the form now known in English as the "limerick," although found in the manuscripts in the common four-line stanza. Two such are included in this collection, the poems to which I have given the titles *The Merry Publican* and *Response of an Angry Customer* (in the mss. the poems are usually untitled, being identified, like the sonnets of Shakespeare, by their first line). Two other poems, not included here, are referred to in the notes to those poems; one of them is by Donncha Rua Mac Conmara, already mentioned as author of the macaronic song and of the long poem *Adventure of Misfortune's Minion*, a poet who had strong links with the Limerick City circle as is explained in the relevant note. These latter poems are dated 1741 and they are in the five-line form now typical of the 'Limerick.'

To trace how the Limerick form went from Irish to English might be beyond the powers of the logical Watson but not of the deductive maestro himself. It is evident that all of those poets were bilingual (see the note on the poem *Response of an Angry Customer*) and some even composed poems in English as did the Kerry poet, Eoghan Rua Ó Súilleabháin (1748-84), author on the one hand of some of the most euphonic and brilliant of the *aisling* or vision poems in Irish, and on the other of the jingoistic ballad, *Rodney's Glory*, celebrating the victory of the English Admiral Rodney over a French fleet in the West Indies in 1782 (a battle in which the press-ganged Kerry poet actually took part) and of a similar ditty praising the Killarney Independent Light Horse, a militia company officered by local landlords. There was also, of course, constant traffic, literary and cultural as well as plebeian and commercial, between Ireland and England in the eighteenth and nineteenth centuries.

Let us hope that in future editions the aforementioned works of reference will look again at the clues already to be found in their current entries on the topic of the now ubiquitous *limerick* form and give some credit to those gifted but unfortunate Irish language poets of Ireland's darkest century, poets unacknowledged and generally unknown in the almost totally anglicised Ireland of today. If that were to be an incidental result of the publication of this collection, I should feel that the labour involved ("A man will turn over half a library to make one book": Johnson) in searching out and translating these poems was more than worth while.

Without wishing to overshadow the poems, which are the heart of the matter, with notes and comment, I have added a brief note on each poem, and a biographical note on the poets (apart from the versatile and prolific Anonymous) which I hope will prove both entertaining and informative.

A final point, and one which could add very much to the enjoyment to be derived from these poems: up to the modern era and the introduction of that formless free verse – which, incidentally, has caused "poets" to proliferate in every country at such a rate as would astonish the *ollamh* (Chief Poet) of the bardic schools where a seven-year course in theory and practice was the normal apprenticeship even to the technical *craft* of poetry, the *art* being left to the Muses or the Divine Spirit to inspire whom they would – all poems in Irish, whether in the strict syllabic form of the bardic metres or in the later stress form (which in Irish is actually classified under the generic name of *amhrán*, literally *song*) were intended to be sung or recited. While the professional *file* (poet) was the acknowledged author of the poem, another professional, the *bard*, was the man who sang or chanted the poem to a harp accompaniment during the banquet in the dining-hall of chief or king (in modern Irish the word *file* is still used for poet, while Scottish Gaelic uses the word *bard*). It will probably come as a surprise to many English readers, as it did to me when I first read John Aubrey's *Brief Lives*, (as edited by Oliver Lawson Dick) to learn that up to the time of the

Cromwellian Civil War the harper-poet was also an important component in the cultural life of at least some parts of England: "When I was a boy," says Aubrey (he was born in Wiltshire in 1625) "every Gentleman almost kept a harper in his house: and some of them could versifie."

Most readers of this book probably have not recited a poem since their schooldays – even in schools the practice is sadly neglected nowadays – or perhaps even since they chanted their nursery rhymes. Apart from the final three poems, the poems in this book beg to be read aloud. It might be dangerous to startle your fellow-passengers on a plane by suddenly starting to declaim *The Woman of Three Cows* or *The Monk's Welcome to the Herring* – the pilot might radio ahead to have the police and the men in white coats waiting for you at the airport. On the other hand, the company might welcome the alternative to thumbing through the airline's magazine or looking at some old film, and you might even be asked for more of the same. In solitude, however, there is nothing to stop you reciting these poems aloud as the poets themselves did – I often imagine that scene when blind Raftery recited his latest composition in some crowded peasant cottage in County Galway, or when the poets of the Maigue Court of Poetry gathered in Seán Ó Tuama's tavern in Limerick to read and discuss their new works. And if you enlist another voice, the second poem in this collection, the serio-comic contention between the missionary Patrick and the old pagan warrior-poet Oisín, comes to dramatic and meaningful life; in fact, it would make an entertaining piece for radio or television. So, having first perused the poems silently as is our modern way, and perhaps given some attention to the meticulous craftsmanship with which they were structured, imagine yourself as the poet reciting the poem aloud for the very first time. The dog may howl, or the cat may wince, but I guarantee that you yourself will enjoy the performance.

Críostóir Ó Floinn.

Oisín's Lament In Old Age

Although attributed to Oisín, the son of Fionn Mac Cumhaill, this poem was probably composed by a poetic monk in some Irish monastery. The writing of poems may have been frowned upon by some of the saintly abbots of such monasteries (an injunction imposed many centuries later on Gerard Manley Hopkins by his Jesuit superiors) but the attribution of the poem to some famous personage, whether mythical like Oisín or historical like Colmcille – who returned from his self-imposed exile in Iona to intercede with the High King of Ireland when the poets were in danger of being silenced because of their use of the satire as a means of extortion – would allow for its preservation in written form. Even the best-known of such poems, in which a monastic scribe compares his cat, Pangur Bán, chasing mice with himself seeking the *mot juste*, was written as a mere *obiter dictum* in the margin of a manuscript in which the poet was dutifully transcribing the epistles of St. Paul. (I sometimes wonder what penance the abbot would have prescribed for such doodling, however artistic). Like Colmcille himself, many monks in the early centuries of Christianity in Ireland were probably trained by the professional poets, and so the ancient bardic lore and poetic skills were thus preserved and passed on to later generations of monastic scribes. Like most of the early Irish poetry, the poem cannot be dated exactly; the original poem might be as early as the 8th Century.

The theme is common enough in all poetry, but in these three short stanzas the poet manages, by the use of vivid imagery and self-deprecating black humour, to convey concisely and vividly the gradual but inevitable metamorphosis wrought by the passing years. The original Irish makes more skilful and euphonious use of alliteration, a favourite device of the poets, than can be done in an English version. In a literal translation, the final line would read: "I am not as I was," which sounds trite without the embellishment of the alliteration and the play on vowel sounds used by the poet in Irish. I have tried to make up for this loss by the use of an image of which I feel our poet would wryly approve.

Criostoir O'Flynn

Oisín's Lament in Old Age

Once I had bright locks that waved
Like corn in golden sway,
Now nothing on my head remains
But stubble short and grey.

A mane as black as raven's wing
I'd much prefer to show
Instead of this grey furry thing
My head can only grow.

Lovemaking is futile for me now,
No more the ladies' man;
To fate this old grey head I bow –
Tonight I'm an also ran.

Caoineadh Oisín Seanóir

Do bhádhas-sa uair
fá fholt bhuidhe chas,
is nach fuil trém cheann
ach fionnfadh gearr glas.

Do ba loinne leam
folt ar dhath na bhfiach
do thidheacht trém cheann
na fionnfadh gearr liath.

Suirghe ní dluigh dham
óir ní mheallaim mhnaoi;
m'fholt anocht is liath,
ní bhia mar do bhí.

The Dialogue Of Pádraig And Oisín

The Poet: Again we have no knowledge of the author of the original poem, and can only surmise that he was a poetic monk who lived in an Irish monastery at some time between the eighth and the twelfth centuries. Besides having the poetic gift and training, he obviously was a born dramatist who never – so far as we know – saw a play, since, for one reason or another, the drama, like the novel, never developed as a feature of native Irish culture. It is possible of course, that monks from Europe could have seen and read the plays of Roman and Greek playwrights, and even native Irish monks might have read some of those plays, perhaps without the permission of the abbot. Many of the poems are cast in the form of dramatic dialogue, and some stories also have very dramatic interludes. The dramatic form effectively makes this poem into a two-hander piece played out on the stage of the imagination.

The Poem: The poem purports to be a dispute between Saint Patrick, a foreign missionary (who had, however, spent six years as a slave in Ireland and so, unlike many missionaries in later times, was fluent in the language and familiar with the culture of the people) and Oisín, the warrior-poet son of Fionn Mac Cumhaill, who was said to have spent three hundred years in *Tír na nÓg* (The Land of Youth) and to have returned to Ireland only to find that Fionn and his army, Fianna Éireann, had all died long before. The poet imagines the old man, Oisín, being cared for by Patrick and his monks, but reluctant to accept their invisible and allegedly almighty God or their strange ways of worship in stone buildings, with much clanging of bells and ritual chanting. I have selected typical passages from what is now a very long and inevitably somewhat repetitive poem, and arranged them so as to form what I hope is an artistic entity which gives the lively polemic and salty humour with which the original poet cleverly sugared the pill of a very serious theme, viz. the coming of Christianity and its impact on the native culture.

THE DIALOGUE OF PÁDRAIG AND OISÍN

OISÍN

Pitiful, Pádraig, is my state
After those great ones left behind,
Listening now to bell-ringing priests
And I needy, old and blind.

If Fionn and the Fianna lived still,
Swift leave of your clerics I'd take,
I'd be hunting the deer in the glen,
A grab at its leg I'd make make.

If yourself with the Fianna had been,
O keeper of crosses and priests,
You'd not bother your head with God,
Nor in churches and schools to teach.

PÁDRAIG

For all in this world I'd not go
From God who o'er all holds sway;
You'll regret, you soft-headed poet,
That you tried to lead clergy astray.

Your boasting of Fionn's gifts of gold
Will be told against him and you too;
Fionn is held captive in hell,
Paying well for the deeds he must rue.

OISÍN

From you now I'll believe not a word,
With your white books come from Rome;
Great Fionn, that generous chieftain,
Neither demon nor God could control.

One hero of the Fianna alone
Would in combat be more than your match;
Your Lord of the holy rule
And yourself, too, he'd soon dispatch.

PÁDRAIG

Oisín of the sharpened spears,
In your speech no sense we find;
Any day God is more mighty
Than your whole fighting Fianna combined

OISÍN

If Conán Maol alive stood here,
Our man whose speech was so vile,
He'd break your head with one blow
Tho' among your priests you might hide.

PÁDRAIG

It's silly of you, poor old man,
Of the Fianna to chant on and on;
You should choose now with God to side,
Your long life is almost done.

OISÍN

It's no wonder I boast about Fionn
When of God's Son you constantly shout;
If he did half the great deeds of our chief
Your priests could be truly proud.

PÁDRAIG

Where are the Fianna now?
Where now their power and their valour?
They have vanished and left no trace;
Good Oisín, take the faith we offer.

OISÍN

Your faith I will never accept,
O miserly cleric so mean;
From Éire all joy has been banished
Since you and your band here appeared.

PÁDRAIG

In Éire there never was joy
Until I and my clergy appeared;
All that came here before then
Are in hell suffering pain severe.

OISÍN

There was indeed joy in Éire,
Great plenty, too, while the Fianna lived;
In those days I wouldn't live half-starved
On scraps like your clerics now give.

PÁDRAIG

The food of the soul is the best,
Oisín, man of troublesome tongue;
Where now the strength of past years
To pursue the swift deer all day long?

Let us both give contention a rest,
Old man so bereft of good sense;
Accept now that God reigns in heaven
While Fionn groans in hell with his men.

OISÍN

It's a shame for your Lord if he rules
Not to free Fionn from the place of pain;
If your God were in need of relief
Our great chief would be first to his aid.

PÁDRAIG

Torment on you, cranky old man!
Your words are a madness as ever;
I have told you, our God is greater
Than all your great Fianna together.

OISÍN

Pádraig of the crooked staff
Your answer rings bold in my ear,
But your staff would in splinters lie
If my fine son, Oscar, were here.

But now, Pádraig, in confidence tell,
If you are so well in the know,
Would your King my dog and my hound
With myself allow into his fort?

PÁDRAIG

Old man, are you raving still?
Not a tittle of sense do you show;
No way can your dog or your hound
Be allowed with you into God's fort.

OISÍN

If to go to that fort you are minded,
O Pádraig who have guided my steps,
I'll accept your faith and your rule
If you'll bring with us Fionn and his men.

PÁDRAIG

The Fianna and Fionn cannot go
With us, Oisín, towards that fort;
They are captives held fast in their chains
In that dark place of pain, as I've told.

OISÍN

Well then, Pádraig, explain to your God
Not to know him was none of their fault;
If they had heard of him while on earth
Gladly they'd have served in his cause.

You can tell him also from me,
If he can't for Fianna Éireann find room,
Let him send me to suffer in hell
With them and my well-loved Fionn.

Criostoir O'Flynn

AGALLAMH PHÁDRAIG AGUS OISÍN

OISÍN

Is trua, a Phádraig, mo scéal:
 mé tar éis na bhfear go fann,
ag éisteacht le cliar na gclog
 is mé im' sheanóir bocht dall.

Dá maireadh Fionn is an Fhiann
 do thréigfinnse cliar na gcros,
do leanfainn an fia fán ngleann
 's ba mhian liom breith ar a chois.

Dá mbeifeása fairis an Fhiann,
 a chléirigh na gcliar is na gcros,
ní thabharfá aire do Dhia
 ná do riar cliar agus scoil.

PÁDRAIG

Ní thréigfinnse Mac Dé Bhí
 ar a dtáinig thoir agus thiar;
a Oisín, a fhile bhoig,
 is olc rachas duit díol na gcliar.

Gach ar bhronnais-se is Fionn d'ór
 is olc rachas dó agus duit;
tá sé in ifreann i ngeall
 mar do-níodh feall agus broid.

OISÍN

Beag a chreidimse ded' ghlór,
a fhir ón Róimh na leabhar mbán,
go mbeadh Fionn an flaith fial
ag deamhan ná ag Dia ar láimh.

Dob fhearr aon churadh amháin
dá raibh ar Fhiannaibh Éireann
ná Tiarna an chrábhaidh
agus tusa féin, a chléirigh.

PÁDRAIG

A Oisín na ngéarlann,
a chanas na briathra buile,
dob fhearr Dia le haonló
ná Fianna Éireann uile.

OISÍN

Dá maireadh Conán Maol,
fear mílabhartha na Féinne,
do bhrisfeadh sé do bhaitheas
istigh i measc do chléire.

PÁDRAIG

Bheith ag sírtheacht thar an bhFéinn,
a sheanóir, is baoth do chor;
cuimhnigh go dtáinig do ré
agus gaibh Mac Dé ar a shon.

OISÍN

Ní hionadh mise do theacht thar an bhFéinn
is tusa thar Mac Dé gan sos;
dá ndéanfadh Sé a leathoiread leis an bhFéinn
ba mhór É ag cléir na gcros.

PÁDRAIG

Cá bhfuil an Fhiann anois?
Cá bhfuil a dtreise ná a dtréin?
d'imigh an Fhiann gan trácht,
is glacsa creideamh, a Oisín fhéil.

OISÍN

Do chreideamhsa ní ghlacfaidh mé,
a chléirigh gan bheith fial,
is gur thréig an sonas Éire
ó thángais féin agus do chliar.

PÁDRAIG

Ní raibh an sonas ar Éire
go dtáinig mé agus mo chliar;
gach a dtáinig romhainn go hÉirinn
atáid in ifreann na ndaor-phian.

OISÍN

Do bhí an sonas ar Éire
is rath mór lenár linne an Fhiann;
ní hé an uair sin do bheadh mise beo
gan mo leath-dhóthain den bhia.

PÁDRAIG

Bia an anama isé is fearr,
a Oisín na gcomhrá ndian;
cá bhfuil do neart ná treise do lámh
nach leanair gach lá an fia?

OISÍN

Ba mhór an náire sin do Dhia
gan glas na bpian do bhuain d'Fhionn,
agus Dia féin dá mbeadh in airc
go dtroidfeadh an flaith thar a chionn.

PÁDRAIG

Cráiteacht ort, a sheanóir,
a chanas na briathra buile;
dob fhearr Dia aon uair
ná Fianna Éireann uile.

OISÍN

A Phádraig na bachaille caime,
do bheir orm freagra dána,
do bheadh do bhachall ina bruscar
dá mbeadh Oscar do láthair.

A Phádraig, inis damh-sa fá rún,
más agat atá an t-eolas is fearr,
an ligfear mo ghadhar nó mo chú
liom go dún Rí na ngrás?

PÁDRAIG

A sheanóir atá ar baois
  is nach fuil ort críoch ná aird,
ní ligfear do ghadhar ná do chú
  leat go dún Rí na ngrás.

OISÍN

Más dearbh leatsa dul don dún,
  a Phádraig, fá lúth triall liom,
leanfad do réim is do rian
  má bheir tú leat an Fhiann agus Fionn.

PÁDRAIG

Ní bhéarfad liom Fionn ná an Fhiann,
  a Oisín, ar mo thriall don dún,
mar atáid i nglasaibh go daor
  is go doimhin i ngéibheann dubhach.

OISÍN

Inis, a Phádraig, don Dia úd
  nach raibh fhios ag Fionn ná ag an bhFéinn
go raibh Sé ann lena linn,
  is dá mb'fhios gur ghnaoi leo dá réir.

Abair leis fós gan dearmad tráth,
  muna ligfidh dá láthair an Fhiann,
mise do chur fán bhFéinn
  ag fulang na péine mar iad.

Dying Of Love

The Poet: The anonymity of the earlier monastic poets may have been due to spiritual causes, but the aristocratic author of this poem had a very different reason for not wishing his name to be known – he is mocking the poems of *amour courtois* (courtly love) which were a popular artistic hobby among the aristocratic poets of all medieval western Europe from their beginnings with the troubadours of Provence in southern France during the 12th century. The theme of unrequited love and the description of the unnamed beauty (who was never, of course, the poet's wife!) were common to those poems; the artistic skill lay in a display of technical expertise and the use of imagery and word-music. The Irish adaptation of this form fitted the basic concept to the native metres. One of the most noted of the Irish poets of courtly love was Garrett Fitzgerald, third Earl of Desmond (1338 – 1398), known in Irish as Gearóid Iarla (Garrett the Earl), a descendant of those Norman invaders who eventually became "more Irish than the Irish themselves."

The Poem: As I have mentioned in my Introduction to this collection, in his introduction to *Dánta Grá* (an anthology of these poems of courtly love edited by Tomás Ó Rathaille) the

Oxford scholar and hibernophile, Robin Flower (translator of *An tOileánach*, Tomás Ó Criomhthain's account of his life on the Great Blasket Island) singles out ironic humour as the distinctive Irish contribution to these poems. The author of the present poem goes further by making ironic mockery of his poem, just as, in a later age, Shakespeare, author of over one hundred and fifty sonnets expressing love for a dark-haired lady or a handsome young nobleman, turned his pen one day to mocking the stereotyped images and similes of his fellow-poets: "My mistress' eyes are nothing like the sun/Coral is far more red than her lips' red/ If snow be white, why then her breasts are dun. . ."

I have adhered in my version to the classical bardic rhyme scheme of the original, which, in addition to the English end-rhymes between the second and fourth line of each stanza, requires a rhyme between the end of the first line and some word inside the second line, similarly between the end of the third line and a word inside the fourth line.

DYING OF LOVE

It's all bad news to the fore!
Ne'er heard of more in battle slain
Than are said now to die of love;
A wonder how I alive remain!

Love for a woman on this earth
I've never felt, that's best by me;
Nor will I ever till Judgement Day,
Enough beneath that sway I see.

These men who say of love they're
dying
Must leave behind them lovely wives;
Gladly they'll listen to myself
If no man else remains alive.

These men are happy so to die;
One in a hundred, I stay put;
Christ, why should I want to die
When of women soon I'll find a glut?

All these you cause in pain to dwell,
If truth they tell, on their last gasp,
For death daily they moan and sigh:
O God on high, grant what they ask!

These simpletons who ne'er
transgressed,
Och! O Mary, fairest of all,
Woe to you, cause of such grief
To those who'd live or die withal.

O Son of Mary, strange the sight,
Men withering with desire of death;
Pitiful simpletons who can't relate
Love or hate with their last breath.

They make themselves a laughing-stock,
In death-pains locked, they loudly
swear;
Announcing they must soon expire:
A fine trick to seduce the fair!

Why should I heed a single soul
Of those who say of love they die
When in their form no change appears?
Take heed, O Christ, of all who lie!

AG DUL D'ÉAG DEN GHRÁ

Aghaidh gach droichscéil amach!
ní chuala mé cath ba mó
ná a bhfuil ag éag leis an ngrá:
is ionadh dhúinn mar táim beo.

Taom grá do mhnaoi fán ngréin
ní thugas féin, feirrde liom,
nocha dtiobhar go dtí an bás;
ní beag liom cách ina ghioll.

Na fir seo ag dul d'éag den ghrá
fúigfid siad na mná dá n-éis;
eadamair éistfidhear rinn
muna bhé beo ach sinn féin.

Na fir shuairce seo théid d'éag,
mé an t-aon de chéad gan dul leo;
a Chríost, créad fáth bhfaghainn bás
's go bhfaghthar mná is anmhain beo!

An lucht so atá uaibh i bpéin,
más fíor dóibh féin, i riocht mhairbh,
léigid míle cnead is uch,
a Dhé, go dtí an guth fán ngairm!

Na daoithe nár pheacaigh riamh,
och, a Mhuire, a chiabh na gclann,
is mairg duitse atá dá mbreodh,
bíodh gur cuma a mbeo nó a marbh.

A Mhic Muire, nach ait dúinn
iad ag seargadh súil re bás?
mo thruaigh daoithe na nduadh,
's nach aithnid dóibh fuath ná grá.

Daoine ag magadh fúthu féin,
dá rá go mbíd i bpéin bháis,
dá bhagair go rachaid d'éag –
ionadh an gléas meallta ar mhnáibh.

Créad fá gcreidfinn duine féin
dá rá liom go dtéid d'éag,
's nach tig claochló ar a chruth?
Fear, a Chríost, ar lucht na mbréag!

The Monk's Welcome To The Herring

The Poet: Of all the poets whose identity is hidden, for one reason of another, under the generic name, *Anonymous*, (in Irish they are known as *File Gan Ainm*, "a poet without a name") the author of this (15th C.?) poem is the man I would most like to meet. In the previous poem, some aristocratic dilettante was expressing scorn for the stereotyped love-poems of others of his kind, but here is a man living in the severe conditions of a Celtic monastery, about to commence forty days of rigid fasting, whose sense of ironic humour can focus on a topic so unpoetic as the salted herring which confronts him as his dinner on Ash Wednesday; from this unpromising material his truly original mind concocts a unique artistic composition. He is a monk, but in the poetic tradition of Colmcille and the other monastic poets. Where he got his training in the rigorous bardic forms, to add to his natural artistic gift as a poet, is one of the questions I should like to put to him. At first one imagines him as a jolly fat friar, but considering that his dinner for the forty days of Lent is to consist of one salted herring, I am more inclined to see him as a tall, gaunt ascetic, but with a twinkling eye and the soul of a born joker. As in the case of the anonymous monastic author of *Pangur Bán*, one can only regret that such a gifted poet probably expended most of his mental energy on tedious spiritual hack-work, making copies of the Scriptures, and dashing off a poetic gem like this only as an afterthought, perhaps to amuse a few of his confrères who were "birds of a feather" in the poetic sense.

The Poem: The matter of the poem needs no comment, but anyone with a relish for wit and irony must find some of the images and *bons mots* in this poem worth savouring. The rhyme scheme is in the same intricate mould as the previous poem; but in the original poem the line is in the old Irish measure of seven syllables rather than in the stress metre of English verse.

THE MONK'S WELCOME TO THE HERRING (On Ash Wednesday)

Dear Herring, that you've come I'm so glad,
Move closer, young lad so well-bred,
Good health and long life may we have,
Fair welcome you're bade and deserve!

I swear by your father's own soul,
Tho' Boyne salmon afford a fine feed,
This verse is for you all alone,
Most noble and youthful of breed.

My fine chap, in your body so smooth,
Never false or untrue in your love,
No friend of your like have I found,
Let no foul play our friendship disprove.

If the nobles of Banba were to judge
The relative worth of these three,
Pike, salmon, or herring, we know
The fine fish that foremost would be.

Adventuring on far foreign coasts
From here to the oceans of Greece,
The hero Conán from Slea Head
Never met with your match in the seas.

O Herring, so merry and mild,
Sound minder of Lent's holy time,
Beloved fair son of loved friend,
To end a long wait you've arrived.

On this dish in the year that's gone by
Many more of your tribe met their doom,
But you harbour no venom or hate,
To us clerics so faithful a boon.

O Herring, so pleasant, so tasteful,
Never baleful in aspect or mood,
To your coming I raise no objection,
With affection this look is imbued.

As Lent penitential begins,
With you I'll drink many a round,
To you, till the Easter sun rise,
'Tis right that my love should be bound.

FÁILTE AN MHANAIGH ROIMH AN SCADÁN

(ar Chéadaoin an Luaithrigh)

Mo-chean do theacht, a scadáin!
  druid liom, a dhaltáin uasail;
do chéad beatha 's do shláinte!
  do thuillis fáilte uaimse.

Dar anam t'athar, a scadáin,
  gidh maith bradáin na Bóinne,
is duit labhras an duain-se,
  ós tú is uaisle 's is óige.

A fhir is comhghlan colann,
  nach ndéanann cumann bréige,
cara mar thú ní bhfuaras;
  ná bíom suarach fá chéile.

Dá bhféachdaois uaisle Banbha
  cia is mó tarbha den triúr-sa,
iasc is uaisle ná an scadán,
  idir bradán is liúsa.

Is é ar bhféachain gach cósta
  go crích bhóchna na Gréige,
iasc is uaisle ná an scadán
  ní bhfuair Conán Chinn-tsléibhe.

A scadáin shéimh shúgaigh,
    a chinn chumhdaigh an Charghais,
a mhic ghrádhaigh mo charad,
    liom is fada go dtángais!

Gidh mór do thit anuraidh
    dod ghaol bunaidh fán méis-se,
ná cuimhnigh fíoch ná fala,
    ós tú cara na cléire.

A scadáin shailltigh shoilbhir
    nach mbíonn go doilbhir dúinte,
liomsa do theacht ní hanait,
    súil ar charaid an tsúil-se.

I dtús an Charghais chéasta,
    a fhir le ndéantar chomh-ól,
ortsa, go teacht na Cásca,
    is mór mo ghrása 's is rómhór.

The Woman Of Three Cows

The Poet: The author of this poem, in addition to being *Anonymous* can be classified under the species *Dispossessed Poet.* With him we come to a turning-point in the history of Irish literature, of which poetry was to remain the sole and deteriorating genre until its lingering death in the early part of the 19th century. It was to experience an artificial resuscitation with the foundation of the Gaelic League in 1893 and the so-called Irish Literary Revival (which eventually did more for English literature through the works of Yeats, Synge, Joyce and others than for the mummified muse of "Dark Rosaleen"). With the defeat of the Ulster chiefs, O'Neill and O'Donnell, at Kinsale in 1601 began the collapse of the whole Irish system of clans and chieftains. These had been the patrons of the bardic schools and of their family's own poet laureate. With the chiefs exiled or dispossessed, or gone over to the English religion and culture, the professional bard was reduced to dependence on the hospitality of the peasantry, that "common mob" for whom the Roman poet, Horace, expressed such distaste.

The Poem: The opening and closing stanzas of this tragi-comic piece make a little poem in themselves, a gem of poetic irony. In between, however, the dispossessed bard inevitably launches into an elegiac litany of the great Irish chieftains who were the munificent patrons of his class, concluding each example with his admonitory refrain (thus making a further technical problem for himself and any translator wishing to keep to his prosodic pattern). In recent times the poem became known in an English version by James Clarence Mangan, the Dublin *poète maudit* of the nineteenth century. Like some modern poets and others who publish so-called translations "from the Irish," Mangan knew little or no Irish and worked from prose translations made for him by scholars. His version of this poem reduces it to a colloquial doggerel: "O woman of three cows, a ghrá/ Don't let your tongue thus rattle/ O don't be saucy, don't be stiff/Because you may have cattle." The reader who does not know Irish should ask someone who does to read aloud the opening verse of the original poem and compare its dignified sonority with that jingle. The final stanza is even worse, untrue to the original and jarring both eye and ear with the banal phrase "I'd thwack you well." In spite of which, Colm Ó Lochlainn, publishing this version in his *More Irish Street Ballads* (1965) praises Mangan for having "bettered the original anonymous Gaelic verses."

THE WOMAN OF THREE COWS

Easy now, woman of three cows!
Don't be so proud of your fine herd,
A woman I know – 'tis no lie now –
Can double that in cows well-fed.

Wealth does not forever endure,
Presume on no-one to look down,
Death comes nearer every hour;
Easy now, woman of three cows!

Great Eoghan's valiant Munster race
Won fame even in their going down,
Their sails by fate brought low;
Easy now, woman of three cows!

Heroic clan of Clare's brave Lord,
Their lost cause a tale of sorrows,
No hope they'll e'er again be seen;
Easy now, woman of three cows!

Dónall of the ships, Dunboy's
O' Sullivan whose voice rang proud,
By sword in Spain cut down;
Easy now, woman of three cows!

O' Rourke and Maguire who were once
In Erin topics of renown,
See for yourself: vanished and gone;
Easy now, woman of three cows!

O' Carroll's clan who strongly stood,
Victors in many a bloody hour,
Not one lives today, alas!
Easy now, woman of three cows!

Having one single cow more
Than your neighbour of two can count,
Last night was your boastful theme;
Easy now, woman of three cows!

Envoy

I swear by my cloak, O lady of haughty glance,
Persistent and prickly in watching for every
chance,
By your setting three cows as the measure of
wealth so grand
If I should get four to own you'd be surpassed!

BEAN NA dTRÍ mBÓ

Go réidh, a bhean na dtrí mbó!
  as do bhólacht ná bí teann;
do chonaic mise gan gó
  bean is ba dhá mhó a beann.

Ní mhaireann saibhreas de ghnáth,
  do neach ná tabhair táir go mór;
chugat an t-éag ar gach taobh;
  go réidh, a bhean na dtrí mbó!

Sliocht Eoghain Mhóir sa Mhumhain,
  a n-imeacht do-ní clú dóibh,
a seolta gur ligeadar síos;
  go réidh, a bhean na dtrí mbó!

Clann gaisce Thiarna an Chláir,
  a n-imeachtsan ba lá leoin,
is gan súil lena dteacht arís;
  go réidh, a bhean na dtrí mbó!

Dónall ó Dhún Baoi na long,
  Ó Súilleabháin nár thim glór,
a thitim sa Spáinn le claíomh;
  go réidh, a bhean na dtrí mbó!

Ó Ruairc is Mag Uidhir do bhí
  lá in Éirinn ina lán beoil,
féach féin gur imigh an dís;
  go réidh, a bhean na dtrí mbó!

Síol gCearbhaill do bhí teann
le mbeirtí gach geall i ngleo,
ní mhaireann aon díobh, fairíor!
go réidh, a bhean na dtrí mbó!

Ó aon bhó amháin de bhreis
ar bhean eile, 'gus í a dó,
do rinnis iomarca aréir;
go réidh, a bhean na dtrí mbó!

An Ceangal

Bíodh ar m'fhallaing, a ainnir is uaibhreach gnúis
do bhíos gan dearmad feargach buan sa tnúth,
tríd an rachmas go ghlacais led' bhuaibh ar dtúis,
dá bhfaighinnse sealbh a ceathair do bhuailfinn tú!

On Miley's Tombstone

The Poet: Like the ironic author of *The Monk's Welcome to the Herring*, this is another man I would like to meet – if only to hear his retort to the snooty comment on his poem by Thomas F. O' Rahilly, sometime Professor of Irish in University College, Dublin, which I quoted in my Introduction to this anthology. Subjective interpretation of literature has its pitfalls even for the scholar of the language, and some of the commentaries I have heard and read make me wonder whether literature can ever be taught except by poets – but then, of course, if the students were to have any hope of passing their exams, the poet-lecturer would have to be restrained from making his lectures into a reading of his own works! The unknown author of these verses was able to use a strict metrical structure not merely for a formal poem such as the poets were obliged to compose for state occasions in the chief's family, but for a dramatic comic poem, something the ordinary poet might even consider beneath his dignity – thus putting himself on the pedantic level of the aforementioned modern academic editor.

The Poem: The metre, as I have pointed out, uses end-rhymes and cross-rhymes with just as much technical skill as is found in the more staid and formal poems of which we have a plethora in the work of the professional poets. But the ingenious use of personification and dialogue bring the poem to dramatic life – which, in spite of the Cup's wry prediction in the final stanza, is more than can be said for the unfortunate Miley who apparently shortened his life by an over-indulgence in drink, tea and tobacco. In spite of Professor O' Rahillys apparent distaste for what he regarded as mere trivia, more liberal lovers of all forms of verse can only surmise as to how many more of such "trivial" pieces were composed down through the centuries, and regret that more of them have not survived. The fact that the metres and diction of Irish classical poetry remained unchanged from the 14th to the 17th centuries makes the exact dating of poems like this a matter of conjecture.

ON MILEY'S TOMBSTONE

A Mug, a Cup and a Pipe
  are here inscribed on his bed;
little they care for Milcy
  who deprived them of sleep and rest.

"I wouldn't mind," says the Mug,
  "if he never got up any more;
'tis often he left my belly
  empty, long day and night o'er."

"The same goes for me," says the Pipe,
   "tho' he often plied me with kissing;
he scalded my mouth every time;
   inside his pocket my head went missing."

"Will ye whisht!" says the Cup,
   "you two dull-wits haven't a clue;
he'll rise hale and hearty enough,
   he's just a bit shook by the booze."

Criostoir O'Flynn

AR LEAC MHAOILRE

Mug, Cupán agus Píopa
  tá anseo scríofa ar a leaba;
is olc a bpáirt re Maoilre,
  nach ligeadh dóibh scíth ná codladh!

"Ní miste liom féin," ar an Mug,
  "ma bhíonn sé gan múscailt choíche;
is minic a d'fhág sé mo bholg
  folamh lá fada agus oíche."

"Mise mar an gcéanna," ar an Píopa,
  "cé gur minic a níodh mo phógadh;
do loisceadh sé mo bhéal gach am,
  is do chaillinn mo cheann ina phóca."

"Éistigí!" ar an Cupán,
  "a dhís breallán gan tuigse;
éireo' sé arís go folláin,
  níl air ach creathán beag meisce."

To A Snorer

The Poet: As the decent man said when thumbing through an anthology of poetry: "That man, Anonymous, must have been a great poet – he has an awful lot of poems in this book." The true poet who composed this poem, and whose identity is hidden forever under that ubiquitous "No-Name," had a sense of humour in the same ironic vein as that of the monk who found material for a poem in his Ash Wednesday herring. Anyone who has ever endured the nerve-racking Chinese torture of listening for the snorer's next drone, whether it be a repetition or a variation on a theme, or who has been made aware of having inflicted that torment on another, will envy the poet both the patient ingenuity with which he has taken refuge in his therapeutic craft and the artistic pragmatism which enabled him to turn an experience of physical and mental inconvenience into a work of literary art that has lasted to be admired and enjoyed by lovers of poetry long after both snorer and poet have gone the way of all flesh.

The Poem: The piece is in the older syllabic form, and is therefore, like similar poems in this anthology, difficult to date precisely, but is probably early 17th or late 16th century. For all his frustration, the professional poet has meticulously structured his poem in the basic classical form, a four-line stanza with seven syllables in each line, an end-rhyme between the second and fourth lines, and a further rhyme between the end of line one and a word inside line two, also between the end of line three and a word inside line four. In addition to the elaborate rhyme scheme, alliteration was also an important embellishing feature of the syllabic poetry – a feature which was retained, sometimes even over-used, in the stress forms adopted by the poets after the bardic schools had disintegrated because of the political and social catastrophe of the seventeenth century. In my English version I have tried to retain the euphonious effect of the rhyme scheme while rendering as vividly as possible the marvellous string of images with which the poet compares the soul-searing sawing to which he is listening while he calmly (?) elaborates his work of art.

TO A SNORER

Your noise by my side is uncouth,
O well-bred youth of rough airs!
That I'd rather you totally dumb
I'm reluctant to bluntly declare.

You'd awaken the dead from the grave
With each soundwave that comes from
  your nose,
O bedfellow stretched at my side,
Hard finding by you my repose.

If either of these menaced me
There would be a lot less to fear
From the woodpecker's boring a tree
Than your snore drilling into my ear.

More melodious the grunting of swine
Than each whine of your nasal tones,
Even sweeter – it can't be denied –
When sand is fine-crushed between stones.

More melodious the call of a calf,
The grate of a clattering old mill,
Or the waterfall's deafening roar
As it foams whitely down from the hill.

More melodious the sea-battered cliffs
Than each snore that drifts out from your
  breast,
Far sweeter the howling of wolves
Than your weird tunes disturbing my rest.

More melodious the ducks on the lake
Than the crake you emit while you sleep,
Seven times sweeter the wave
That comes breaking to shore from the
  deep.

More melodious the bellowing of bulls
Or a dull-sounding bell roughly rung,
Or the head-splitting wail of a child:
All are milder to me than your tune.

Women in labour lamenting
With no hope of let-up from pain,
Wild geese that cry in bleak night
All sound lighter than your nosey strain.

The screech of a knife scraping brass
Can pass with less pain through my head,
Or the grating of cartwheel on stones
Than your deep tones that rattle my bed.

The crash of the waves on ships' sides,
Fierce hounds to the skies howling long,
A thousand times sweeter they sound
Than each round of your chest's strained
  song.

No hope now remains of repose,
On my scalp your snores stiffen the hair,
Every bellyful blowing from your head,
By Brigid, 'tis agony, I swear!

DO SHRANNAIRE

Ní binn do thorann rem thaoibh,
 a mhacaoimh shaoir na bhfonn ngarbh!
giodh deacair dúinn gan a chleith,
 do b'fhearr liom thú do bheith balbh.

Do dhúiseofá mairbh a huaigh
 leis gach fuaim dá dtig ód shrón;
a chaomhthaigh luigheas im ghar
 is doiligh damh bheith dod chóir.

Dá mbeadh ceachtar díobh im chionn,
 do ba lugha liom de ghuais
gáir chaoilcheann ag tolladh chrann
 ná do shrann ag dul im chluais.

Binne liom grafainn na muc
 ná gach guth lingeas ód shróin;
binne fós – ní bhiam dá cheilt –
 gaineamh agá meilt i mbróin.

Binne bodharghuth lag laoigh,
 díosgach drochmhuilinn mhaoil bhrais,
nó géis gairbheasa chaor mbán
 re lingeadh do lár tar a ais.

Binne bloisgbhéime na n-all
 ná gach srann dá dtig ót ucht,
's is binne donál na bhfaol
 ná gach claon chuireas tú id ghuth.

Binne guth lachan ar linn
  ná glothar do chinn id shuan,
agus is binne fá seacht
  fuaim garbhthonn ag teacht i gcuan.

Is binne búirtheadh na dtarbh,
  gáir chlogán, giodh garbh an dord;
gol linbh, giodh siabhradh cinn,
  is binne linn ná do ghlór.

Mná i n-iodhnaibh go ngoimh ag gol,
  gan árach ar sgur dá mbrón,
caoi chadhan in oíche fhuair
  is binne ná fuaim do shrón.

Sgeamhghal sgine re sgrios práis
  ní mheasaim gur páis dom cheann,
ná géim cairte re cloich chruaidh,
  ón dord tig uait ar mo pheall.

Ceannghail tonn re creataibh long,
  uaill fearchon, giodh lonn a sian,
is míle binne céad uair
  ná gach fuaim lingeas ód chliabh.

Árach ní fhaghaim ar shuan,
  do tógadh leat gruag mo chinn;
gach bolgfadhach tig ód cheann,
  dar Brighid, dar leam, ní binn!

The Yellow Bittern

The Poet: This is the first poem in the collection for which an author can be named; unfortunately, although like other poets of the eighteenth century there are many folk-tales about Cathal Buí Mac Giolla Ghunna (anglicised McElgunn) little is known of him except that he was probably born in County Cavan and that, as he himself tells us in this poem, he was "fond of the drop". To this failing he humorously attributes the jaundiced colour of his skin, which caused him to be known as *buí* (yellow), when he compares himself to the bird he laments. He lived in that most dismal of centuries in Irish history when the Penal Laws ensured that the Catholic majority in Ireland were denied official schooling, access to the professions, and practically all legal rights. The towns were garrison towns, totally controlled by the Protestant English and Anglo-Irish. Today some Irish cities, even the capital Dublin, include an area still known paradoxically as "Irishtown." This was originally the shanty town outside the walls to which the "mere Irish" were obliged to retire at curfew. Literature in Irish continued to be confined to poetry and the narration of the ancient stories, and the impoverished and socially downgraded poets began to compose in the more facile modern stress metre of English and other European languages. Any poet was lucky if his poems survived at best in manuscript form, at worst in the oral tradition of the locality to be written down in the next century, often in much corrupted form, by scholars and collectors.

The Poem: The wry self-deprecatory humour of the poem does not hide the tragic personal and national circumstances in which a natural song-bird (appropriate image!) like Cathal Buí had to use his artistic gift. But this piece survives as his memorial. It is still one of the most popular of Irish poems, both as poem and song. The versatile literateur and academic, Daniel Corkery (see note to *Tulyar* by Seán Ó Ríordáin) based a one-act play in Irish on this poem and its author.

THE YELLOW BITTERN

O Yellow bittern, it grieves me to see you lying
Stretched out stiff, all frolics now suspended,
Nor was it hunger brought about your dying
But lack of drink that left you here upended.
I could endure the tale of Troy's destruction
Better than seeing you dead on this bare expanse,
For you were no cause of rapine or of ructions,
No wine you sought but water got by chance.

O lovely bittern, what torment overwhelming
Finding you supine as I wend my way,
When many's the day I used to hear you yelping
Out on the mudflats drinking without care.
Your brother Cathal is warned by all and sundry
That I too will die much sooner than I think,
But that's not true: see here a bird so wondrous
Recently deceased for lack of a drop to drink.

O youthful bittern, 'tis like a thousand sorrows
To see you stretched out cold near bushes bare,
And know that rats are rushing from their burrows
To feast and frolic at your winter wake.
If only you had sent me out a signal
That you were distressed and in such weak
    condition,
On frozen Vesey lake I'd soon come digging
The saving hole to let you wet your whistle.

'Tis not your fancy birds that I'm lamenting,
Not blackbird or thrush or heron do I rue,
But my yellow bittern who cheered me with his
    chanting,
So like myself in habits and in hue.
Ever and always he was fond of drinking,
And so am I, if what they say be true,
Never a drop I find but I'll be sinking,
To die of thirst is what I'll never do.

My darling begs me to desist from quaffing
If I don't wish to exit quick and soon,
I counter that her gab is wayward waffling,
That life is lengthened by this pleasant booze.
Behold the bird whose fine throat clearly rang,
By thirst laid low all in his youthful prime,
So drink up now, good neighbours, while you can,
No drop you'll get when doleful Death calls "Time!"

AN BONNÁN BUÍ

A bhonnáin bhuí, 'sé mo léan do luí
Is do chnámha sínte tar éis do ghrinn,
Is chan easpa bidh ach díobháil dí
A d'fhág in do luí thú ar chúl do chinn.
Is measa liom féin ná scrios na Traoi
Tú bheith 'do luí ar leacaibh lom',
'S nach dtearn tú díth ná dolaidh san tír,
'S nárbh fhearr leat fíon ná uisce poll.

A bhonnáin álainn, 'sé mo mhíle crá thú
Do chúl ar lár amuigh romham sa tslí,
'S gurb iomaí lá a chluininn do ghrág
Ar an láib is tú ag ól na dí.
'Sé an ní deir cách le do dhearthái r Cathal
Go bhfaigh' sé bás mar siúd más fíor,
Ach ní hamhlaidh atá, siúd an préachán breá
Chuaigh in éag ar ball le díth na dí.

A bhonnáin óig, 'sé mo mhíle brón
Tú bheith sínte fuar i measc na dtom,
Is na luchaí móra ag triall 'un do thórraimh
Le déanamh spóirt agus pléisiúir ann.
Is dá gcuirtheá scéala fá mo dhéin-sa
Go rabh tú i ngéibheann nó i mbroid gan
 bhrí,
Do bhrisfinn béim duit ar an loch sin
 Bhéasaigh
A fhliuchfadh do bhéal is do chorp istigh.

Chan iad bhur n-éanlaith atá mé ag
éagnach,
An lon, an smaolach, nó 'n chorr-ghlas,
Ach mo bhonnán buí, bhí lán den chroí,
Is gur chosúil liom féin é i nós is i ndath.
Bhíodh sé go síoraí ag ól na dí,
Is deirtear go mbím-se mar sin seal,
Níl aon deor dá bhfaighinnse nach ligfinn
síos
Ar eagla go bhfaighinnse bás den tart.

'Sé d'iarr mo stór orm ligean den ól
Nó nach mbeinnse beo ach seal beag gearr;
Ach dúirt mé léi go dtug sí an bhréag,
'S gurbh fhaide mo shaolsa an deoch úd
d'fháil.
Nach bhfeiceann sibh éan an phíobáin
réidh,
A chuaigh in éag den tart ar ball,
Is a chomharsain chléibh, fliuchaíg' bhur
mbéal
Óir chan fhaigheann sibh braon i ndiaidh
bhur mbáis.

The Brandy

The Poet: In the ancient bardic schools of poetry, the craft was often hereditary, so that in the history of the literature certain families are associated with poetry just as others might have been connected with the carving of high crosses or the making of chalices, croziers and other works of the goldsmith's art. The fact that the two brothers and the son of this present poet were also poets indicates that this tradition survived for a time after the formally organized bardic schools had ceased to exist. Some forty poems by this poetic quartet have been garnered from the mss. and published in an anthology. Perhaps an indication that they may have been the descendants of some professional bard is the full name of the poet as given in some sources, Diarmuid Mac Domhnaill mhic Fhinghin Chaoil (Diarmuid son of Dónal son of Finian the Slender). This three-generation title also, of course, helps to distinguish this particular Diarmuid Ó Súilleabháin from the many others of that hereditary name in the historic O' Sullivan clan of County Cork (a modern writer of that name was the novelist, poet and dramatist, Diarmuid Ó Súilleabháin, 1932-1985, whose death deprived modern Irish literature of its most experimental writer).

The Poem: Like the previous poem, this piece

also shows the acceptance by the poets, in this transitory period, of the less formal structure which may have been in use already in popular songs. The piece is also another indication of the versatility of the poets in making a poem out of the casual happenings of everyday life. The poet's reason for refusing his relative's Christmas invitation, viz. that bitter experience has taught him to fear the demon Brandy, makes painful humour out of his reluctant asceticism. The heading on the final stanza, *An Ceangal,* literally means the *tie* or *bind,* implying that this concluding stanza summed up the theme and import of the poem.

THE BRANDY

(The Co. Cork poet, Diarmuid Ó Súilleabháin, 1680 – 1750, was invited, in verse, by his friend and fellow-poet, and perhaps relation, Eochaidh Ó Súilleabháin, to spend Christmas A.D. 1729 with him and his family. He sent this poem in reply).

Dear friend, than whom I love no better man,
I vow I'd gladly come, weak as I am,
To visit you in friendship e'er another year start
If I didn't fear the brandy that would lay me flat.

It's no comfort that detains me, nor troubling debt,
Nor the weakness that could cripple an old
grey-head yet,
I'm not afraid to cross rough hills with great rocks
set,
But I fear that by the brandy I'd again be bet.

Bad friend to every soul, 'tis an enemy of God,
The strongest bodies it can bring to lie beneath the
sod;
From Styx's hellish waters that brandy was begot,
A venomous snake that left me oft a senseless clot.

Even the little child who yet has sense to gain,
If he treads on hot embers or suffers any other
pain,
In all his toddlings after he'll avoid that flame,
And that's why I from brandy-boozing must
refrain.

Envoy

O hearty friend, so full of mirth and fun,
Your wife nor you I have no cause to shun,
Across those rugged hills I'd gladly come
But I know that by the brandy I'd be done!

AN BRANNDA

(File i gContae Chorcaí, Diarmaid Ó Súilleabháin, fuair sé cuireadh i véarsaíocht, óna chara agus a chomhfhile – gaol freisin, b'fhéidir – Eochaidh Ó Súilleabháin, i ngeimhreadh na bliana 1729 teacht agus an Nollaig a chaitheamh lena theaghlach. Ag seo an freagra fileata a sheol sé ar ais).

A dhalta dhil dár radas-sa m'ansacht dian,
Geallaim duit go rachainn-se cídh fann mo rian
'Ot fhaicsin-se le carthannacht in am gach bliain
Ach ar eagla bheith trascartha ag an mbrannda
thiar.

Ní seascaireacht fé ndeara dhom ná clampar fiach,
Ná anbhfann do chrapfadh mé, mo cheann cidh
liath,
Ná seachaint dul thar garbh-chnocaibh ramhra liag,
Ach ar eagla bheith trascartha ag an mbrannda
thiar.

Eascara do gach anam é agus namhaid do Dhia
Do leagas coirp dá chalmacht gach ball 'na mbiaid,
Glaise Styx is aisti stilleadh brannda riamh,
Nathair nimh' nach annamh thug mo cheann gan
chiall.

Is cleachtadh leis an leanbh beag cé gann a chiall,
Nuair shatalas ar aithinn ná ar a shamhail de phian,
Go seachnann an lasair sin gach ball dá thriall,
Is ní taise dhom roimh ragairne an bhrannda thiar.

An Ceangal

A shuairc-fhir ghroí do ghní an greann is an sult,
Ní fuath dot mhnaoi ná díbh thug mall mo dhul,
Ná fuath don tslí cé coimhtheach ramhar na cnoic
Ach fuath mo chroí do bhíos don bhrannda agam!

Cock-Eyed Mary

The Poet: Art Mac Cubhthaigh was one of those Ulster poets who, unlike their counterparts in Munster, lamented the demise of their local chiefs, the O' Neill, to whom they had looked, rather than to the exiled Stuarts or the Kings of France and Spain, for the restoration of the old Gaelic order. With the violation of the Treaty of Limerick by the Penal Laws against Catholics (laws denounced by no less a person than Dr. Johnson), the early half of the eighteenth century witnessed the nadir of the social and economic degradation of the native Irish. The poets of this century had to earn their living as best they could; they also, as already noted, abandoned the classic syllabic metres of the bardic schools and began to use the popular stress form, as in English, but with a much more elaborate internal assonantal rhyme scheme which it is impossible to reproduce in English without a ridiculous artificiality. Unknown to the literati of colonial Dublin and London, and at a time when the works of Swift were being published in book form, the poems of these native Irish poets were merely written down and recited at "courts" or gatherings of a group of poets. Many of these mss. were inevitably lost or destroyed in subsequent times. Art Mac Cubhthaigh is one of those poets of what Daniel Corkery called the "Hidden

Ireland" whose handful of extant poems indicates a talent which must have expressed itself in many other works now lost.

The Poem: The Rev. Terence Quinn, parish priest of the Creggan in County Armagh where Mac Cubhthaigh lived, and his sister/housekeeper, Mary, who suffered from a blemish in one eye, were notorious for their greed and for currying favour with likely sources of income in money or kind. When the poet called at the house one day, he was received on the level of a beggar, confined to the kitchen with a bowl of buttermilk, while some more prosperous visitor was treated to wine in the parlour. This satire, with which the poet duly took his revenge and in which he evokes the memory not only of the local O' Neill chiefs but of their prehistoric ancestor, resulted in his banishment. He spent some time working as a gardener in Howth, near Dublin, before being allowed back to his native parish – after he had composed a poem praising Mary Quinn's great beauty!

COCK-EYED MARY

Coloured ribbons adorn all the poor children's
raiment,
The dead are interred without levy or payment,
But of yarn and thread and seed-corn there's a
scarcity
And no butter is rolled but for that Cock-Eyed
Mary.

Every mean little wretch out of misery upraising,
From Legmoylan or the Land of O' Neill his
wealth grazing,
Once the flax is well spun and the praties are
taking
Gets his bottle of wine with that Cock-Eyed Mary.

With no handsome young hero will she ever tarry
Who'd give her a squeeze and sweet kisses so
merry,
But some grubber who pokes out each roundy dark
praty
You'll find drinking the punch with that Cock-
Eyed Mary.

But MacCooey was not fit for a seat at her table,
In the kitchen with buttermilk the poet she stabled,
While the boor, to all learning and culture
contrary,
Gulped wine in the parlour with that Cock-Eyed
Mary.

If the heir of great Colla for this land was caring,
To belittle the poet no one would be daring,
And no scrounger who lives by manure-boxes
making
Would feast in the priest's house with that Cock-
Eyed Mary.

But alas! down in dark earth Aodh Bwee's son is
battened
Nor has man of his match in his place e'er since
happened,
That he lies 'neath a stone leaves our sad hearts
bewailing
But makes life the more pleasant for that Cock-
Eyed Mary.

Our Church's good leader, Doctor Blake, kind and
caring,
We pray to have strength and success in his faring,
Soon he'll cure all the ills that leave good folk
aweary
And he'll settle the swagger of that Cock-Eyed
Mary.

Criostoir O'Flynn

MÁIRE CHAOCH

Tá ribíní daite ar gach páiste istír,
Tá na mairbh dá n-adhlacadh gan cháin gan chíos,
Níl aon nduisin nó cúta le fáil, nó síol,
Níl aon mheascán dá dheisiú ach do Mháire
Chaoich.

Níl aon síogaí beag díblí fuair ardu ó léan,
Ó íochtar Lag Maolain go Clár Uí Néill,
Ach an líon a bheith snímhte 's na preátaí réidh,
Nach bhfuigheadh buidéal fíona aige Máire
Chaoich.

Chan ógánach dóighiúil a b'áin léithe féin,
A phógfadh go ró-dheas nó d'fháiscfeadh léi,
Ach fear a' chróinín chruinn cornuithe as lár na cré
'Sé d'ólfadh an *punch* ró-dheas le Máire Chaoich.

Charbh fhiú léithe Mac Cubhthaigh 'chur ag bord
'na shuí
Ach ins an chlúid is é ag diúl na bláithche síos,
Is an bodach gan oiread den léann le tor fraoich
Ina an pharlús ag diúgadh le Máire Chaoich.

Dá maireadh sliocht Cholla an dá gheal-chrích,
'Sé nach léigfeadh an dán dá chloí;
'Sé nach léigfeadh lucht déanta na mbarrdóg daor
Bheith ar féasta i dtoigh cléire aige Máire Chaoich.

'Sé mo dhíomdha mac Aodha Buí bheith sparrtha i
    gcré,
'S gan aon ar bith diongbháil le fáil 'na dhéidh;
'Sé a shíneadh faoi liag a d'fhág cách faoi léan
'S d'fhág aoibhneas istír aige Máire Chaoich.

Go rabh buaidh 'gus treise i ngach ard den tír
Do n-ár nUachtarán eaglaise, an Blácach caoin;
'Sé 'smachtfadh an droch-stát a bhíos gnách istír
Agus shócairfeadh an góic ag Máire Chaoich.

They're Best Left Alone

The Poet: This poet, mentioned in my Introduction as author of the doggerel ballad in English, *Rodney's Glory*, is known in the folklore of his native County Kerry as "Eoghan an Bhéil Bhinn" (Sweet-Tongued Owen). His *aisling* (vision) poems, in which the poet sees Ireland in the guise of a beautiful lady in distress, who hopes for the coming of the Stuart or some other deliverer, are among the most eloquent and euphonic in what became, for obvious reasons, one of the most popular poetic genres in that Irish-language Ireland of the eighteenth century which was unknown territory to Swift and his fellow-literati in Dublin and London. One of the most melodious and moving of Eoghan Rua's aisling poems was composed while he was on sentry duty as an unwilling recruit in the British army. How he later turned up as a participant in a naval battle in the West Indies is one of the intriguing mysteries with which the poorly-chronicled lives of the Irish poets abound. Another of his best *aisling* songs was composed while he sat in a ditch watching his fellow-labourers engage in some game after they had all slaved a long summer's day as *spailpíní* (hired workers), saving the hay for a farmer near Mallow in County Cork. The word *rua* (red) in his name was commonly used to distinguish a person whose hair was of that fiery hue. In spite of his popular soubriquet, Eoghan Rua could prove as acerbic as any of the other poets. Once when he was preparing to go to a dance, he gave his only pair of stockings to be darned by a woman named Cáit Ní Laoghaire. When the poor woman refused to hand them over until the impecunious poet paid her a fee of fourpence, he gave her instead a lifelong cause of regret in a blistering satire which she would have paid much more than fourpence to have blotted out from the oral repertoire of her neighbours. Like the English dramatist, Christopher Marlowe, Eoghan Rua met his untimely death as the result of a quarrel in a tavern.

The Poem: The piece has little originality and needs no critical comment, being the sort of thing Eoghan Rua could obviously dash off in between downing a few bumpers; but it has a rollicking vigour and moves with the facile eloquence which also typifies his more artistic *aisling* poems.

THEY'RE BEST LEFT ALONE

My verdict I give on all rakish behaviour
Though wayward as any myself I must own,
With soft talk and blather beguiling the favour
Of high-coiffured beauties my kisses made moan;
In secret I shaped my fine verses with labour
That pleased them when murmured in soft, tender tone
And led them on quickly to taste sinful pleasure
Though clergymen teach that they're best left alone.

When in taverns often I sat almost senseless
With a bevy of beauties all drinking galore,
Of the holy men's teaching and threats not a sentence
Had a place in my speeches but mockery and more.
My wages I squandered, I spent many a sixpence
On fiddlers and pipers of excellent tone,
With my mind so elated by chat and enchantment
No man could convince me they're best left alone.

Not a town or a city or seaport in Erin
But some maidens my coaxing have ruefully known,
And if some were reluctant to yield to endearments
I broke their resistance with swearing high-flown.

Had a beauty that morning her vows been
declaring
Even that would not stop me from having a go,
And the holiest bishop with all his great learning
Would not make me agree that they're best left
alone.

A long time I lived in that style quite contented,
In taverns on beauties I scattered my store,
My name often called when accounts were to
render
For the whiskey they swallowed that went on
my score.
In the morning the folly I often lamented,
Of drinking the profit my days could have
shown,
My mind with confusion was then so tormented
I could well have believed that they're best left
alone.

When cross fellows come at me their money
demanding,
Waving bills in their paws for the sums that I
owe
And swearing they'll have me in prison remanded
Though I'm but a poor bachelor whose clothes
are a show,
There's not one of those fair dames who oft had a
hand in
My purse for provision of boozing and sport
But mocks at the trouble in which I am landed:

Then I know, tho' too late, that they're best left
alone.

When approaching old age by my weakness gives
warning,
Not a stitch on my back and not sure where I
go,
The shakes paralytic in limbs every morning,
My words without sweetness, my voice weak
and low,
Bitter thoughts about beauties my mind then is
forming,
All I spent in the taverns gives me reason to
groan,
I declare and admit, with good judgement
concording,
It's a damnable trade and they're best left
alone.

So let all gallant heroes who now play the part
Of drinking in taverns with beauties so bold
Give ear to my warning and take it to heart
If they'd not be infirm and poor when they're
old:
Go and marry a woman who knows the true art
Of loving and caring, whose virtue is known,
Avoid all carousing, all fairs where fights start,
And believe those who tell you they're best left
alone.

Carousing on whiskey and punch at high price,
Then flirting with damsels in beauty full-blown,
Seducing one sweetly, then by some device
Passing on to another, the first you disown;
In secret composing a verse neat and nice,
Breaking heads at the fair but by drink overthrown,
That's the style of the rake, and now here's my advice:
I'm all for it still! They're *not* best left alone.

Criostoir O'Flynn

B'FHEARR LIGEAN DÓIBH

Sin agaibh mo theastas ar bheatha gach réice
Cidh fada mé ag géilleadh le seachmall dá nós
Go bastalach bealaithe ag bladar le béithibh
Na gcarnfholt réidh is dá mealladh le póig;
Aganfhios ag breacadh gach aiste le héifeacht
I labharthaibh séimhe ba thaitneamhach leo
Tré a dtagaid go tapa chun peaca do dhéanamh
Cé teagascaid cléire go mb'fhearr ligean dóibh.

Níorbh annamh mé sealad 'san tabhairne traochta
Idir scata geal-bhéithe le carrbhas óil,
Teagasc na n-aithreach n-aitheantach naofa
Ní thagadh im bhréithribh ach magadh 'gus
móid;
A nglacainn de rachmas ón tseachtain go chéile
Do scaipinn gan séanadh ar scata lucht ceoil,
Bhíodh meanma ar m'aigne is aiteas dá n-éisteacht
Is ní chreidfinn ó éinne go mb'fhearr ligean
dóibh.

Níl cathair ná baile ná caladh in Éirinn
Nár chaitheas-sa tréimhse ann ag mealladh ban óg
'S an ainnir go tapa dom chleasaibh ná géilleadh
Do shladainn a héifeacht le spalpadh na móid;
Níor pheaca liom masla do thabhairt do chéithlinn
I gceangal na cléire bheadh snaidhmithe ó ló,
Is do theagasc an easpaig ba bheannaithe téxa
Bí dearbh ná géillfinn go mb'fhearr ligean
dóibh.

Do leanas na bearta so sealad go séanmhar
'S i dtabhairne ar bhéithibh do scaipinn mo stór
'S m'ainm dá ghairm as leabhar an éilimh
Níorbh annamh nuair a ghlaoinn a gcuid beathuisce ar scór;
Ba chathach mé ar maidin ag machnamh gur bhaoth-bheart
Dom amhail-se d'éagonn mo thairbhe d'ól
Bhíodh m'aigne ag caismirt is mheasainn a séanadh
Go gcreidinn ar éigean nárbh fhearr ligean dóibh.

Is deimhin go dtigid ar buile 'na dhéidh sin
Gach nduine acu ag éileamh 's a bhille 'na dhóid,
Is tugaid na mionna go gcuirfid mé i ngéibheann
Cé singil droch-éadaigh mé ar uireasa stóir;
Níl finne-bhean mhiochair den fhoirinn seo léanaigh
Mo chiste, le géilleadh dá bhfriotalaibh spóirt,
Ná briseann fá scige go scigiúil scléipeach
Ansan tuigim, cé déanach, go mb'fhearr ligean dóibh.

Nuair a thigeann an laige is a dhruideann an t-aos liom
Mé ar uireasa an éadaigh, is chaillim mo threoir,
Bíonn pairthis chreathach gach maidin im ghéagaibh
Ní blasta mo bhréithre is níl tathag im ghlór,

Is searbh an aiste liom labhairt ar chéithlinn,
    Tig an tabhairne séanaim inar chaitheas mo
        stór,
Dearbhaim, admhaim feasta agus géillim
    Gur damanta an chéird í is go mb'fhearr ligean
        dóibh.

Glacadh gac faraire fearamhail saordha,
    A charann na béithe is a leanann an t-ól
Mo theagasc-sa feasta go gasta le chéile
    'S ní heagal bheith aosmhar dó in easpa go
        deo;
Snaidhmeadh le mascalaigh mhaiseamhail
        mhaorga
    Bhéas carthannach caomhnach módhmhail
        leanbach sóch,
Seachnadh dramanna is caismirt ar aonach
    Is creideadh ó éinne go mb'fhearr ligean dóibh.

Carrbhas dramanna beath-uisce is daor-*phunch*
    'S luí ar mhagadh 'na dhéidh sin le mascalaigh
        óig,
Scata acu a mhealladh is le cleasaibh a séanadh
    'S a malairt chun scléipe do tharraing go nódh;
Aiste do cheapadh fá thearmann éigse
    Is caismirt ar aonach tré mhearathal óil,
Sin reachta le rabairne a leanann gach réic bhocht:
    Dá mbearta san géillim is ní fearr ligean dóibh!

Protestant Or Papist

The Poet: Aindréas Mac Craith, known to his poet colleagues as "An Mangaire Súgach" (the Merry Pedlar) was a contemporary of the Ulster poet, Art Mac Cubhthaigh. He was a leading member of the group of poets known as the Maigue poets (from the local river Maigue, a tributary of the Shannon) who met in the tavern of Seán Ó Tuama in the village of Croom in County Limerick. Mac Craith was the Brendan Behan or Dylan Thomas of the group, while Ó Tuama was more in the mould of W.B. Yeats or T.S. Eliot. When the Parish Priest denounced him as a danger to the virtuous women of the parish, Mac Craith took revenge by currying favour with the local Protestant minister; but this move backfired, as he admits in the poem. Eventually he moved ten miles away to a parish where the priest, himself a poet, had a more liberal view. There he composed his euphonious and haunting "exile" poem, *Slán Cois Máighe* (A Farewell to the Maigue) which is still sung and played all over Ireland.

The Poem: Having been thrown out by both the Catholic and the Protestant clergy, Mac Craith jocosely appeals for advice to his close friend and fellow-poet, Seán Ó Tuama, and declares that he will be forced now to join some strange sect like the Arians. But he also manages to remind the

Christian clergy that Christ's attitude to sinners was not the same as theirs, and his use of Christ's challenge to the Pharisees seems to imply that the priest and the minister were themselves not above reproach in their personal lives. Like Art Mac Cubhthaigh in County Armagh, Mac Craith eventually settled back into the Catholic fold. Ironically, when as a sick old man he felt the approach of death, the now unmerry pedlar sent an appeal, in the form of four stanzas, to the parish priest in the nearby town of Kilmallock, asking him to get the ailing poet to the hospital. He then set out to walk to the town, but was overcome by weakness as he reached the first house, owned by a family named Hawthorne descended from a County Down Presbyterian who had married a local Catholic girl and become a Catholic himself. He was taken in and died sitting in a chair at the fireside. The family had him buried in their family grave and at their own expense.

PROTESTANT OR PAPIST

Dear friend, do you regret to hear the fix I'm in,
Thrown out by clergy, without cause dismissed?
To be nothing but a tramp I'm considered fit,
They won't accept me as Protestant or Papist.

One of them calls me a chancer extraordinary
Who claimed that I was English to get on his list,
When I blurt out that going to Mass I'd rather be,
But consider myself neither Protestant or Papist.

He then declares that I must be arrested
And brought to court for trial – and he insists
He'll find some way to have me truly tested,
For I must needs be Protestant or Papist.

The priest declares my peddling ways seductive,
Calls me a sharp-tongued, indiscriminate satirist,
Worse than an outlaw, he says, at raising ructions,
And he won't have me, Protestant or Papist.

An outsider, without shame, he also chants me,
My deeds and ill-fame put me on his black list,
I'm nothing but an impecunious ranter
Who practises being a Protestant but no Papist.

Neither charity nor love of satisfaction
Such denigration before foreigners permits;
No credit to him, such abusive action,
No matter whether I be Protestant or Papist.

Since now I find myself from church an outcast,
Wandering homeless, confused in my poor wits,
I'll have to join with the opposite of that class,
They'll take me, whether Protestant or Papist.

Though Magdalen and King David both were long
    astray,
And the apostle who put many on his prison list,
They were not spurned when they changed their
    ways,
And none of them was Protestant or Papist.

Dear friend, where do you think I should wander
next,
Since, not knowing why, in error I exist?
I'll have to join the Calvinists, or that Arian sect,
Having done with being Protestant or Papist.

And now let any of those of whom I've told you,
Who never strayed or sinned, take in his fist,
The stone to throw and aim it at me true,
Whichever I be, Protestant or Papist.

Envoy

See the Apostle who sinned thrice in a row
Denying his Friend, how he was then forgiven:
Dear God, bad as my sins may show,
Along with Peter let the Pedlar into heaven.

PROTESTAN NÓ PÁPAIRE

A dhalta dhil an danaid libh mo chás anois,
Dom chartadh tiubh, ag eaglais gan fáth ar bith;
An aicme sin ní ghlacaid mé ach im fhánaire,
'S ní ghabhaid liom im protestan ná im pápaire.

Deir pearsa acu gur cearrbhach neamh-ghnáthach
mé
'S go n-admhaim gur Sasanach do láthair mé,
Nuair scaraim leis chun Aifrinn go mb'fhearr liom
dul,
'S nach ceachtar mise protestan ná pápaire.

Dearbhann gan dearmad nach foláir leis mé
Do chartadh tiubh le harma do láthair chirt,
Go rachaidh liom chun achrainn gan spás ar bith
'S go gcaithfead bheith im protestan nó im pápaire.

An sagart deir gur feannaire neamh-fhálach mé
'S go dtarraingim le mangaireacht na mná chun
oilc,
Gur measa mé ná ceatharnach atá le broid,
'S ná glacfaidh mé im protestan ná im pápaire.

Is do freagradh gur eachtrannach gan náire mé,
Is nach taitneamhach mo bhearta ná mo cháile ris,
Nach atharrach mé ach reacaire atá gan strus
Do chleachtann bheith 'na phrotestan 's nach
pápaire.

Ní carthannacht fé ndeara dhó ná grá do shult
Mo chartha-sa do thagradh do láthair Scoit,
Ní maise dhó mo mhasladh-sa i gcás ar bith
Pé acu mise protestan nó pápairc.

Ó caitheadh mé as an eaglais is go dtarla amuigh
Is gur fada mé ar mearathall gan áit ar bith
Caithfead cur le hatharrach na táine sin
Do gheabhas liom im protestan nó im pápaire.

Cé fada do bhí Magdalen is Dáibhí an *king*
Ar mearathall is an t-aspal do chuir táinte i mbroid
Do glacadh iad nuair chasadar i gcáil 's i gcion
Is ceachtar díobh níor phrotestan ná pápaire.

A chara dhil cá rachad-sa chun fáin anois?
Ós feasach mé ar dearmad gan fáth gan fios,
Caithfead bheith im Chailbhinist nó im Árian oilc
Ó scaras le bheith im phrotestan nó im pápaire.

'Bé acu den aicme-se ar a dtráchtaim-se
Nár dhearmaid na haitheanta is atá gan choir
Caitheadh liom a gharbh-leac go hábalta
Pé acu-san mé protestan nó pápaire.

An Ceangal

Féach an t-aspal do pheacaigh fá thrí ar dtúis
Ag séanadh a Charad gur glacadh arís go humhal;
A Dhé dhil aitchim, cé scaras le dlí na nUrd,
Mar aon le Peadar an Mangaire scaoil it dhún.

The Merry Publican

The Poet: Already mentioned in the note to the previous poem, Seán Ó Tuama was the central figure in the school or court of poets who flourished in County Limerick in the eighteenth century, one of many such groups which were the poor heirs to the great bardic schools of poetry. Ó Tuama's modest tavern in the village of Croom was a natural meeting-place for the poetic court. Ó Tuama himself was an affable personality who managed to keep on good terms with all classes and creeds; some of the local Protestant landlords even sent their sons to be tutored by him – like many of the other poets he kept a small school and was himself a classical scholar, conversant with the ancient Greek and Roman literatures and fluent at least in Latin. In spite of his social and diplomatic talents, Ó Tuama, like many of his fellow poets, suffered many disturbances in his personal life – one of his poems laments his fate in being reduced to acting as poultry-keeper for the termagant wife of a farmer. He later moved to Limerick City, where he again tried his hand as publican, opening near the Mungret Gate in the historic walls of Limerick a tavern which soon became a gathering place for the poets. He eventually returned to die in his native village of Croom.

The Poem: Ó Tuama obviously dashed off this

short piece as a lighthearted celebration of his profession as innkeeper; but it has become an item of unusual literary interest for other reasons. Firstly, it was the cause of what must be the most tragic row in the history of Irish literature. Ó Tuama, possibly urged thereto by his managerial wife, Muirinn, refers obliquely in the poem to some customers who were not keeping their slate clean. This was taken as a personal insult by his bosom friend, the volatile Aindréas Mac Craith, who – so the folk legend says – was the owner of the longest slate, amounting to one guinea. The next poem is Mac Craith's violent repsonse. Ó Tuama did not reply, although other poets did so on his behalf – causing Mac Craith to issue an even more virulent poetic retort in which he linked Ó Tuama with Judas and notorious traitors in the recent Jacobite wars. Sadly, the two old friends never spoke to one another again. Secondly, taken together, these two poems are evidence, as I have pointed out in the introduction to this collection, for what seems self-evident, viz. that the verse-form now known as the "limerick" is so called because it originated in Limerick.

The Merry Publican

I'm a person who daily sells drinks
And my company sets to high jinks,
But I say, by the way, if some one fails to
  pay,
It's **my** loss when the account sinks.

Drink the brandy to your best endeavour,
By the inch your good cloth never
measure,
The best of the wine for a shilling is mine
And the growlers we'll tolerate never.

I delight in the airs of the harp,
In songs and in sport to take part,
To see Muirinn, my lass, filling up the
bright glass
And with friends of good sense to share
chat.

Reciting the poets ancient store,
Playing cards, drinking brandy galore,
While talented players perform pleasant
airs,
That's how I enjoy life evermore.

An Tabhairneoir Meidhreach

Is duine mé dhíolas leann, lá,
Is chuireas mo bhuíon chun rangcáis,
Muna mbeidh duine ar mo chuideachta dhíolfas
Mise bheas thíos leis in antráth.

Taoscaidh bhur ndóthain den bhranndán,
Bhur n-éadaí ná tómhaisíg' le bannlámh,
Tá agamsa scilling le leigean 'san bhfíon ghlan
'S is fearra ná an bhuíon ag dranntán.

Do b'ait liomsa ceolta na dteampán,
Do b'ait liomsa spórt agus amhrán,
Do b'ait liomsa an gloine ag Muirinn dá líonadh,
Is cuideachta saoithe gan meabhrán.

Ag aithris eolais na sean-dámh,
Carrbhas, ól agus branndán,
Foireann an ghliocais ag seinm na laoithe –
Siúd mar do ghnímse gach antlás.

Response Of An Angry Customer

The Poet: The note to the poem *Protestant or Papist* identifies the talented but unpredictable author of this piece.

The Poem: Although not written in the five-line stanza which is now used for the "limerick," the metre and rhyme-scheme of this and the previous poem flow naturally in that form. The content of the poem needs little comment, except that it does seem to indicate a guilty conscience – but also sadly reveals something of the indignation and frustration of the impoverished poets of this dark century, who were even more degraded socially that the poets of the previous century, like the author of *The Woman of Three Cows*. A later poem in which Mac Craith replied to those poets who attacked him because of this present piece begins with a preamble indicating that Mac Craith suspected the hand of Ó Tuama himself in their defence of his old friend; it is prefaced with a virulent preamble in Irish, in prose and verse, followed by this curious paragraph in English which, however regrettable its tone, at least indicates that these poets were more than fluent in English as well as Irish: "If you are so reduced as not to show a farthing in your poetical purse, turn broker and get your living as Mahara did, or rather, as auctioneer, sell the lumber out to public sale to those about you, such as old shoes, bristles, stinking fish and the like; or if you choose, turn rag-gatherer, porter, or common scullion, clear the streets of rubbish. Better do so than turn affidavit man and swear you saw or heard what you did not."

The poet whom his poetic colleagues in the Croom Court of Poetry had lovingly called "The Merry Pedlar" then launches into his second poetic attack on Ó Tuama, a poem of eleven stanzas, all, of course, impeccably constructed and embellished with alliteration and the other ornaments of the poetic craft!

RESPONSE OF AN ANGRY CUSTOMER

You're a man who sells drink by the splash,
Your brandy and ale are a mash,
All who drink your bad booze their memory
lose
And their brains are confused in a hash.

Furthermore, the tricks up your sleeve
Your customers often deceive,
Not a man but you make his good sense to forsake
With your gab and your grumbling so peeved.

Your lays and old poems are as sour
As the drink that you splash as you pour;
Too much of the glass stays unfilled by your lass
And your punch was ditchwater before.

You daily sell slops as fine drink,
Filled by Muirinn well short of the brink,
And we justly complain at your boastful claim
That by this we are set to high jinks.

How often you've poured the short measure
And topped tankards with froth at your
    pleasure,
Then left us unfit to stand or to sit
Or to make our way home at our leisure.

Domineering at the head of the table,
Your own tankard to empty well able,
But if anyone else is short a few pence
You torment the whole house with your raving.

It's true you come fawning to meet
Every gent who comes strolling the street,
But if he gets a glass without paying hard cash
It's *his* loss when your bill his eyes greet.

He'll get no parting glass, that's for sure,
Without money or a pledge that's secure,
And he'll have to pay, tho' he run where he may
Or fall into a ditch sick and sore.

It's the topic where'er good men discuss,
That your sly ways make this country worse;
For more drink in your well you and "Slippery"
    would sell
The very customers who fatten your purse.

My heart's love the great poets of old times,
Not like Seán of the sly cunning wiles,
Like a tyrant insane, his madness is plain
And his bosom breeds nothing but lies.

Every mirth-seeking man of our throng,
Every poet and weaver of song,
Who to Limerick may come, let him instantly
 run
To be welcomed where I now belong.

From *this* host, whom you'll never hear grouse,
And his lass, a demure gracious spouse,
We have punch in a stream and wine like a
 dream
And with free ale we daily carouse.

CUSTAIMÉIR FEARGACH AG FREAGAIRT

Is duine thú dhíolas steanncán,
Buisinn gan bhrí 'gus branndán,
Is cuireas do chuideachta ar uireasa cuimhne
'S a n-inchinn líonta de mheabhrán.

Is deimhin arís go meallfá
Go minic do bhuíon le sleamhnán,
'S go gcuirir gach duine ar giodam chun baoise
Le gliogar gan chríoch is le cannrán.

Níl binneas it laoi ná it shean-dán
'S ní milis dar linn do steanncán,
Bíonn iomad de thuise do ghloine gan líonadh
Is d'uisce na díge it phonnseáin.

Buisinn dá dhíol mar leann, lá,
Ag Muirinn dá líonadh i ngann-cháirt,
Ní sultmhar don fhoirm seo sibhse dá insint
Go rithid dá bhíthin chun rangcáis.

Is minic do líonais lom-cháirt
Is coirn fá mhaoil le cúbhrán,
Is cuirir-se sinn-ne gan chumas ar shuidhe
Ná imeacht san tslí gan teanntán.

Cé mursanta shuidhir ag ceann cláir
'S go n-ibhir leath síos gach tanncárd,
Muna mbeidh scilling ag duine chun díola
Cuirfir do bhuíon chun stanncáird.

Tigir, is fíor, le lútáil
I gcoinne gach n-aoin dá ngabh' an tsráid,
Gloine má thugair do dhuine gan díol
Is i mbille bheidh thíos air in antráth!

Ag n-imeacht dó arís an deamhan cárt
Do-gheibhidh gan díol nó gealltán;
Is cuma cá h-ionad 'na rithfidh, cá díg
Ina dtitfidh fá thrí ar a lamhancás.

Ní chluinim ag dís 'na gcomhrá
Ach go millir an tír le sleamhnán;
Slibire an Droichid is sibh-se go ndíolfadh
Ar ghloine nó ar dhís bhur gcompán.

Cuisle mo chroí na seann-dáimh
Ní h-ionann is dlaoithe mheang-Sheáin,
Mursaire buile tá ar mire dá ríribh
'S a bhruinnibh gur líonta d'fhallsán.

Gach duine den bhuíon ler bhfonn ábhacht,
Gach file, gach saoi le hamhrán,
A thiocfa go Luimneach, ritheadh gan mhoill
Go sconnaire an ghrinn le ngabhaim páirt.

Siollaire groí gan cannrán
'S a mhuirineach mhín-tais mhodhail mná
De bheir *punch* do gach duine ina shrutha 'gus
    fíon
Agus coirn gan díol de leann bhreá.

The Adventure Of Misfortune's Minion

The Poet: Like several other poets, the colour of his hair added the descriptive word *rua* (red) to the personal name of Donncha Mac Conmara. He was born in the village of Cratloe in County Clare, some six miles north of the city of Limerick. In one of his poems he refers to Limerick as "Áit ar shloigeas go minic piontaí mo dhaethin" ("a place where I often drank my fill of pints"). He must surely have frequented that tavern "at the Mungret gate" and met up with Seán Ó Tuama, Aindréas Mac Craith, and other poets from the converging counties of Limerick, Clare and Tipperary. He is said to have studied for the priesthood at the Irish College in Salamanca; later he spent some time in Newfoundland, where he wrote what has become the best-known of exile songs in Irish, *Bánchnoic Éireann Óighe* ("The Fair Hills of Holy Ireland"). Eventually, Mac Conmara settled in County Waterford where he kept a school. He outlived all the other poets of his circle, and his long life provided the novelist, Francis MacManus, with material for a trilogy of novels. His death in 1810 was fulsomely noted in several newspapers, one account concluding thus: "His compositions will be received and read until the end of time with rapturous admiration and enthusiastic applause."

Alas, in the Ireland of today his name and work are practically unknown.

The Poem: This rollicking account of the poet's abortive attempt to emigrate to America has led some critics to deduce that the plaintive exile poem mentioned above was actually composed in County Waterford! Others are of the opinion that the poet made a second successful venture across the Atlantic, to Newfoundland. The poem may well have been the model for Merriman's better known *Cúirt an Mhéan Oíche* (The Midnight Court) which it preceded by thirty years or more. The poets were contemporaries, both natives of the same general area in County Clare. The poems are in the same metre and style, and both contain a dream sequence featuring Aoibheall na Craige Léithe, queen of the local fairy fort, in this poem as the poet's guide through the Underworld, in Merriman's as the severe judge of the nightmare court before which the bachelor poet is arraigned. This poem shows that acquaintance with the classics which was common to the Irish poets of the eighteenth century: Mac Conmara even indicates the kind of poetry written by each of the Roman poets he encounters in the Underworld. My version is based on the text as given in the two editions of Donncha Rua's poems by Risteard Ó Foghludha (1909, 1933) rather than on that of Tomás Ó Flannghaile (1892) which is longer by some eighty lines but less cohesive. Reading either this poem or Merriman's, one feels that, given the time and leisure such as Milton and

Dante enjoyed, these Irish poets could have produced an epic in Irish to match *Paradise Lost* or the *Divina Commedia*.

THE ADVENTURE OF MISFORTUNE'S MINION

Tales I could tell on many a theme
That pleasant to all ears would seem,
Of Brian Boru, of Fionn and his Fianna,
McLobe's mean mob and his cousins meaner,
But these must wait while I relate 5
The misfortunes heaped on myself by Fate.
Being short supplied of this world's wealth
And seeing poor Ireland in such bad health,
No rent, no help, but false possession,
Racked by this foreign tribe's oppression, 10
Teaching school was the work of my days
And the world knows that's an empty trade,
One night in bed as I lay alone
I wondered what life had yet in store,
The years going by with nothing to show 15
Far better were spent in service low,
In charge of horses or carting the soil
With my fill of fresh milk like Malachy's boys.
If I left old Ireland now, I thought,
As a clerk I might start a new life abroad, 20
With fair wind in my sail I'd make my way
To New England far across the sea.
When the morning came from the bed I leapt,
Still pleased with the plan I made ere I slept,
I grabbed my stick and off I dashed 25
With a stylish ferk to the rim of my hat.
Short jackets were made in the wink of an eye,
Striped shirts with sleeves to the fingers' lie,

To my friends I bade a fond farewell
But with time so short some I missed as well. 30
Unless ships in Ireland could not be found
I'd cross the sea to a safer ground.

That decent folk of Power's fair land
Came offering me a helping hand,
Brought food, utensils, all kinds of ware, 35
Enough to survive in storm or war.
Provisions that many a day would maintain
And a trunk that could myself contain.
There were seven stone of oats well-sieved
And what leavings the kneading-trays could give, 40
A barrel of praties, Ireland's finest,
For fear the hungry days might find us,
Seven score eggs of hens and others
For eating whenever the mood came on us,
A big jar of butter packed tight by labour 45
And a salted joint of weight and savour.
I'd a keg of beer that would flame with one puff,
Dead men would rise to taste that stuff.
Bed and bedclothes rolled together
Tightly to my trunk were tethered. 50
I had boots and a wig and a beaver hat
And even more on top of all that.

To Waterford then I straight proceeded
Bold as the Fianna's Conán the fearless.
I got bed and board in the best of style 55
From a damsel the fairest in Erin's isle.
She had curling locks and a smile so sweet
And in drawing a drink she was pleasant and neat.

So pretty, lively, so tidy and bright
Her stories and chat were a constant delight. 60
Not a cross word or look would she ever bestow
As long as she knew you had funding galore.
Of her womanly ways I must now be discreet
But her wink made my heart with joy replete.
Of my deeds she broadly spread the fame, 65
With her own hands powdered my manly mane.
First thing in the morning I'd a drink in bed,
She barbered me neatly from toe to head.
A wonder she was in her welcoming way
While her Ma wouldn't hold for a penny's delay. 70
That miserly mother not a drop would dispense
Till my cash in her hand covered all the expense.
With them I lingered day by day
Awaiting a ship to take me away.
It was then Captain Allen, a hearty man, 75
Arrived in town and we soon shook hands.
I got myself ready all in a rush
With my goods and as much as I'd left in funds.
On a carrier's nag to Passage I rode
With a load of herrings to balance my load. 80
My trunk went on board with no bother at all
While the harbour gents were having a ball.
I was asked if English I could speak,
In Latin I answered, muddled and meek,
Officially then the clerk my name took, 85
I wrote *Mac Namara* in the Day Book.
My trunk and myself were placed side by side,

We had music and merriment all the while.
We sailed when noon was marked by Phoebus,

Aeolus and Thetis both being gracious. 90
To the open sea they made good speed
And travelled far out in the sun's great heat.
Poor Manus and family soon looked wry
At the rolling sea and the spacious sky.
Tadhg O'Leary had ready his carrots and whey
But no drop nor bite could he stomach that day. 95
Then Kielty O'Keefe began wailing his wife,
No way could his heart be consoled in this life.
Just as Lawlor's young lad was saying grace on his
grub
He got knocked in the eye when Calvagh
threw up. 100
Gerald and Tibbett and Gerard were trying
To pull out my plug while the others were dying,
And Diarmuid observed with a face full of pain
That not one man in three would see Ireland again.

That's how they were in the dumps a fair while, 105
Exhausted, dejected, deflated, destroyed,
And I swear I was nothing the better myself,
In misery stretched, as sick as the rest,
Like a lifeless felled ox with no hope of relief
Or an empty old sack giving never a squeak. 110
Alas and alack, all my joking was gone,
I was market-place butt, the fair's common clown.
To the merciful God my prayers were not slack
That a storm to Ireland would turn us back.
More than all I had seen or could ever be offered, 115
More than Croesus the King had of wealth in his
coffers,

The gold fleece that Jason brought back, as we
read of,
The stores of the Scots and of greater Dalriada,
Or to win as a prize beauteous Deirdre the fair
By whom Uisneach's brave sons were doomed to
their fate, 120
More than George left in Flanders of money and
store
When to Hanover home he escaped from his foes:
All these I'd exchange, without hesitation,
To be safely at home or in any safe haven,
To be back in the Barony, 'mid good Irish stock 125
Dispensing my verses and ruling my flock,
Or once more with that priest, my tutor so kind,
Tasting generous refreshment for body and mind,
To be back on Slieve gCua unsurpassed for its
welcome
To all makers of magical song and their helpers, 130
Near to William O'Moran, that sage of high mind,
Who'd lament me in classical style if I died.

Through all those thoughts of my troubled mind
There came a fairy woman mild,
Her flowing locks to earth did flow, 135
Her rosy cheeks were all aglow,
From her figure and face I could plainly see
It was Aoibheall, the magic queen of Craglea.
This gracious sibyl led me away
Till by a smooth green lawn we stayed, 140
A cave that moaned like stormy weather
I saw near a thorny bush and heather.
I pondered my case, this situation:

Was I being led into more frustration?
She answered my question before I could ask, 145
"Don't be anxious or angry at this my task;
The things of this world must not amaze you:
Just stay by me and you're in no danger;
No men of Thomond ever observed
The sights I'll show and that you deserve." 150

Together we descended out of sight
Into that cave in the broad daylight,
And came to the bays of a bitter sea
Where Acheron cold flowed at our feet.
To this dismal swamp come those who die, 155
Every soul and spirit, condemned on high.
Thousands dolefully there were gathering
Who could not cross for want of bartering:
Not as of Aeneas Virgil tells
That the body had not been yet interred. 160
Now I'd often heard scholars asserting sagely
That the boatman there was Charon the scaly;
I tell them now they're a lying clan:
He's a big strong lump of an Irishman!
Busy in that old boat we've seen you, 165
My gallant loner, Conán of the Fianna!
The ewe's black fleece on his big backside
Made him easy for us to identify.
For each English soul he charged sixpence pricy
And spoke not a word but in Latin or Irish! 170
When he spotted myself in Aoibheall's care
He looked a fright and wagged his bald pate,

Like a bull he bellowed fierce and loud:

"You wrinkled miserable hag, so proud
That you dare a man still alive to guide 175
To this place where no sliver of flesh can abide!
If I felt like displaying the power in me tethered
I'd batter yourself and your fellow together!"
"Easy, my hero!" said the mild majestic,
"Curb your temper, be more receptive: 180
This harmless man I found in sore trouble
Is a scion of Ireland's great and noble."
That lad then grabbed my fingers tight
And roared with laughter and delight,
His bellowing shook the skies above us, 185
Hell moaned as it echoed through the universe.

We crossed the stream in his little black currach,
By short cut went towards a small grassy hillock,
We came to dark swamps and an unlocked gate
Where a dog should be raising his howl of hate. 190
For Virgil tells true when he says in his verses
That here was the fierce and implacable Cerberus.
He was sound asleep in the middle of our way,
Snoring and snorting, on pea-straw he lay.
That Irish hero, a mighty man, 195
Gripped his throat with his powerful hands,
The brute couldn't turn or twist an inch
While we ran past by terror pinched.
Nor did we stop till we reached that hill,
And there we rested and looked our fill. 200
I saw crowds of folk in every direction
Coming and going with force and friction.

He told us then to sit and listen

While he explained each group's condition.

"See yonder men of our Irish race," 205
Said he, "and ladies our land did grace;
The heroes of Greece and Troy do you see?
Hector with his sword, boasting his deeds,
Ancient Anchises, worn and grey,
His son at his side and their famous forbears. 210
Do you hear this racket from the poets' mob?
At their music and sport and gab without stop!
Horace there making fun for Maecenas
Cutting those others with sharp-edged verses;
Ovid alone on a grassy mound 215
Composing his notes to Caesar proud;
Between his fingers Juvenal grips
A pen in poison and vinegar dipped:
There's our Irish poet, Aodh Mac Cruitín,
His Gaelic verses sweetly singing; 220
Their modest master in mirth and glee,
His songs from death would set men free!
Over there, alas, see the Fianna's host,
That fearless, swift, unvanquished force.
Alas! great Fionn, once in command, 225
If we were back in our native land
Brave Charlie his way home would find
With Scots and Irish force combined.
Look now on Luther who changed the ruling,
And furious Calvin, their fat is oozing; 230
And there's Henry the Eighth with his queen
unlawful
Chained in the stocks in anguish awesome.
But all those you see who roam unbound

Will pass one day to God's holy ground.
Now you go home," said that hero powerful, 235
"And in Ireland you can make announcement
That the gentle scion of James will reign
As King defending your people's claim
Till a son of our ancient native strain
Arises the upper hand to gain, 240
Who will wrest the crown from George deceitful
Restoring the line of great Milesius.
Avoid what caused Eve's seed such loss,
Pray, and fast, and carry your cross,
With alms and true love help the poor 245
And a place in heaven you'll ensure.
I must be off, they're shouting and bawling!
This Luther's lot have my insides crawling.
In multitudes the French have killed them
And across to this side I must ship them." 250

With a mighty leap he vanished away,
Then gently Aoibheall took me in care,
Up here I know not how we returned,
Like a rabbit pushed with a pole from its burrow.
Suddenly I woke from that slumber deep 255
On my bed, my trunk and clothes at my feet,
And felt myself dizzily thrown around
With the ship heading fast for English ground.
My torment nothing less did seem
That the terrors I'd suffered were only a dream. 260

A cry went up, "A sail, a sail!
The hammocks all down, odzouns she'll take us!"
A neat French frigate, swift and well-gunned,

Had forced us in terror from her to run.
She fired a blast across our bows 265
Her forty guns all booming loud,
She made us turn as fast as could be
For if speed couldn't save us our fate was sealed.
As the hound chases after the hare o'er the grass,
Trapping and turning, both trying to outlast, 270
Till the hunter must halt if she runs out of puff,
That was our battle – and that was enough!
There were twenty men killed of our crew in that
game,
Many more of them wounded, mangled and lame,
Three died as the day o'er the sea was dawning, 275
Another fifteen lay in agony moaning.
The bullet that wounded the Captain's young brat
Paid him back for his deed when he stole my fine
hat.

We got back to Passage all battered and sore
And I made for Waterford all on my own. 280
On a ship I'll ne'er go for the rest of my life
Unless beaten on board or with ropes tightly tied.
Now to end all my tale, to Christ I give thanks,
My friend when in need, O King by us stand,
Forgive us and strengthen and bring us to glory, 285
Our souls ever helping – that's all my story.

EACHTRA GHIOLLA AN AMARÁIN

Do riarfainn sceól dom chomharsa ar aon rud
I mbriathra beoil dob eol do chéadta,
Ar Bhrian Bóirmhe, ar shlógh na Féinne,
Ar chliar mhic Lóbais, fós a ghaolta,
'S níor chóra dhom teacht thar dreas dá saothar 5
Ná ar nódhacht do bhain dom d'easpa an tsaoil seo,
De bhrí go rabhas-sa gann fí ghréithre
'S gur fríoth go fannlag dream na hÉireann,
Gan chíos gan chabhair ach speannsas bréige
'S da gcíoradh ag clann na ngall so is tréine. 10
Ag múineadh scoile dob obair dom laethibh,
'S a rún don phobal go mb'fholamh an chéird sin.
Ins an oíche im luí 's mé im aonar,
Dom seal ag smaoineadh ar íde an tsaoil seo,
Ag caitheamh mo bheatha gan earra gan éanrud, 15
'S go mb'fhearra go fada bheith tamall mar mhaol
  bheag
I gcomhar na gcapall nó ag cartadh na cré seal
Nó ag ól bainne i dtigh M'leachlain Uí Mhaona,
Nó fós go rachainn as talamh na hÉireann
'S go mb'eol dom sealad do chaitheamh im
  chléireach, 20
'S go rachainn fí sheol le feóithne ar séide
Go Sasana Nódh más dóigh go mb'fhéidir.
Ar dteacht do mhaidin do phreabas go héadrom
As mo leaba le taitneamh an scéil seo,
Beirim ar mhaide 's ní stadfainn ar aon chor, 25
Is feilc ar mo hata san bhfaisean is faobhar air.
Déantar *jackets* bheag' ghearra le sméide

Is léinteacha breaca go barra mo mhéara.
Do chuir mé slán lem chairde in éineacht
Is ag cuid níor fhágas slán le foréigean. 30
Dá gcasadh gan árthach a d'fhagháil in Éirinn
Do rachainn thar sáile in áit nár bhaol dom.

Fiadhain ar ghlacas ó mhaithibh sin Phaorach
A liacht beatha, mion-earra agus gréithre
Do thug an pobal i bhfochair a chéile 35
Chun ár gcothuithe i gcogadh nó i spéirlinn,
Stór ná caillfeadh suim de laethibh
Agus cófra doimhin a dtoillfinn féin ann;
Do bhí seacht gclocha 'mhin-choirce glan-chréithre ann
Is dríodar crochta na loiste le chéile, 40
Is lán an bharaille b'fhearra bhí in Éirinn
De phrátaí leathana d'eagla géarbhroid;
Do bhí seacht bhfichid ubh circe agus éanla ann
Le haghaidh a n-ite chomh minic 's ba mhéin linn;
Cróca ime do dingeadh le saothar, 45
Spóla saille ba throime 's ba mhéithe;
Do thugas ceaig leanna ann do lasfadh le séide
Is chuirfeadh na mairbh 'na mbeatha dá mb'fhéidir,
Leaba agus clúda i gciumhais a chéile
Ceangailte ar dhrom mo thrúnc le téadaibh; 50
Bhí bróga istigh ann, *wig* is béabhar
Agus stór mar sin anois ná déarfad.

Go Port Láirge den stáit sin téimse
Comh farránta le Conán na Féinne;
Glacaim mo lóistín bord bia is féasta 55
Fairis an ógmhnaoi ba chóraí in Éirinn.

Do bhí sí fáinneach, fáilteach, tréitheach,
Ba chaoin deas sásta an *drawer* le glaoch í,
Ba ghleoite, b'aibidh, ba ghasta, bá néata
D'inneosadh eachtra, startha agus scéil duit; 60
Ní ghlacfadh sí fala ná fearg go héag leat
An feadh bhraithfeadh sí airgead agat gan
traochadh;
I gcúrsaí mná ní thráchtaim éanrud,
Ach cúis mo gháire fáth a sméide;
Do rinn sí mo chlú dá mb'fhiú mo shaothar, 65
Do chuireadh sí im chúl-sa púdar glégeal;
Bhíodh deoch ar maidin 's mé im leaba dá gléas
dom,
Ó bhun go barrra 'sí bhearradh go léir mé.
Ba mhór é m'iontas a soineantacht féile
Is cruas a muime chun pingne d'éileamh: 70
Ní mhaithfeadh a máthair cárt ná braon dom
Go gcaithfeadh sí an táille d'fháil gan phlé uaim.
D'fhanas 'na bhfeighil sin suim de laethibh
Ag fuireach le loing do rachadh as Éirinn.
Bhí Captaen Ailín, fear meanmnach aerach, 75
Ag teacht don mbaile 's níorbh fhada gur réidheas
leis.
Gléasaim orm go hobann le féirsce,
Mé féin is mo chostas ar sodar in éineacht.
Chuas don Phasáiste ar ghearrán le caraeire
Is ualach scadán 'om mheáchan ar thaobh de. 80
Do chuaigh mo chófra ar bórd go héasca,
Is uaisle an phóirt ag ól gan traochadh.
D'fhiafradh go haibidh an labhrainn Béarla
'S d'fhéadas a bhfreagairt i Laidin ar éigin.

Níorbh fholáir dom m'ainm do thabhairt don
  chléireach, 85
Is *Mac Namara* chuir trasna sa *Day Book.*
B'éigean mo chófra sheoladh ar thaobh díom
'S mé ag éisteacht ceoil is spóirt in éineacht.
Scaoiltear seolta ar nóin do Phoébus,
Do bhí Aeólus leo agus Thétis: 90
Scinnid de phreab amach san tréanmhuir,
Druidid abhfad i dteas na gréine.
Níorbh fhada gur ghoill ar chlainn sin Mhaonais
An fharraige dhoimhin is radharc na spéire.
Bhí meacain is meadhg ag Tadhg Ó Laoghaire 95
Is ní bhlaisfeadh sé greim le treighid ná braon de;
Bhí Caoilte Ó Caoimh ag caoineadh a chéile
'S ní bhfaigheadh a chroí bocht scíth ar éanchor.
Bhí buachaill Uí Leathlobhair ag altú a bhéile
'S cé bhuail é sa leathshúil ach Calbhach is scéird
  air; 100
Bhí Gearailt is Tiobóid is Gearóid ar saothar
Ag tarraingt mo phlocóide in onóir na scléipe;
Gur dhearbhaidh Diarmuid thiar go faobhrach
Ná mairfeadh a dtrian le triall ar Éire.

Sin mar do chaitheamar tamall go taomnach, 105
Tuirseach, atuirseach, treascartha, traochta,
Is bíodh ar m'fhalaing nár thaise dom féin sin,
Sínte tarsna chomh hainnis le héinne.
D'fhanas im mhart gan phreab gan faothamh
Mar a bheadh sac gan fead gan glao ionam; 110
Mo chreach fada, ní magadh ba mhéin liom,
Im chleas margaidh 's im lastram aonaigh ;
Ba mhinic é m'iarraidh ar Dhia, dá mb'fhéidir,

Stoirm dár bhfiaradh aniar go hÉire.
B'fhearr ná a bhfeaca de mhaitheas an tsaoil 115
Is é d'fháil, cé fairsing, a raibh i dtaisce ag
  Croesus,
Ná an lomra órga thóg mac Jason,
Ná sochar na Scótach is mór-Dháilréada,
'S dá bhfaighinn 'san imirt an fhinnebhean Déirdre
Ler cailleadh clann chumasach Uisneach na dtréan-
each, 120
Nó ar dhearmad Seóirse i bhFlóndras de ghréithre
Ag teacht óna nómhaid go Hanover ar éigean:
A ndeirim do thabhairt mar mhalairt le buíochas
Ar bheith sa bhaile nó i gcalathphort éigin,
Ar bheith san mBarúnaigh 'om neartú idir
  Ghaelaibh 125
Ag reic mo cheathrún 's ag smachtú mo thréada,
Nó fairis an sagart thug teagasc go séimh dom
Is blaise na leanna go fairsing gan éileamh,
Nó ar Shliabh geal gCua rug bua na féile
Ag riar lucht duanta, druadh, 's a gcléirigh, 130
Farra Uilliam Ó Moghráin fonn-árd léannta
Do chanfadh seanndán os ceann chláir m'éaga.

Ar lár mo smaointe is m'intinn traochta
Do tháinig an tsíbhean mhíonla mhaorga,
A cuacha scaoilte síos go féar léi, 135
A grua mar chaoir ag suíomh a scéimhe;
Ar íoghair a pearsan a d'aithin mé ar éigean
Aoibheall chleasach na Craige Léithe.
Do tharraing an fháidhbhean mhánla léi sinn
Gur stadadh linn láimh le báinsigh réitigh: 140
Chonnacas uaigh a ngluaiseadh gaoth as,

Sceach ar a bruach lastuas is fraoch glas.
Do mhachtnaigh mé an cás go hárracht éadmhar,
'S cé'n t-achrann fáin 'narbh áil léi mé chur.
Do thug sí go haibidh freagra in éiric: 145
"Ná cuireadh beart ar bith fearg ná fraoch ort;
Ná déan iontas de nithibh an tsaoil seo;
Ná treig mise go bhfillead, 's ní baol duit;
Radharc ná fuair fir Thuadhmhan is léir
Go bhfaighirse uaimse is luach do shaothair." 150

Buailimid i ngeimheall a chéile
'San uaigh sin síos ar shoilseadh an lae ghil,
Go bhfeacamair uainn ann cuanta is géar-mhuir
Is Acheron fuar ag gluaiseacht taobh linn.
Seo an t-eanach 'na ngabhaid an dream so éagann 155
Gach anam is samhail i ngeall a daorthar.
Na mílte ceann bhí ann go déarach
Ná faighheadh dul anonn thar abhainn le réiteach:
Ní hionann mar thiteann ó Virgil le hAenghus –
Gur le huireasa a gcurtha ar an tsaol so. 160
'S é chloisinn dá rá ag lucht ráite is léinn
Gurab é duine bhí i mbád ann Cháron méirscreach:
Adeirimse leo gur dóibh is bréag san –
Ach cleithire mór de phór na hÉireann.
Do chímís i seanbhád thú dá tiomáint go
saothrach, 165
A dhíthreabhaigh ghalánta, a Chonáin na Féinne.
Do bhí craiceann dubh fóisce ar a thóin mar éadach
'S beag linn go deo air mar chomhartha an méid sin.
Nó thabharfadh Sasanach tarsna gan réal gheal
'S ní labharfadh dada ach Laidean nó Gaeilge! 170
Nuair a chonaic sé Aoibheall bhinn is mé aici

Crothann a mhaoil 's ba scíosmhar a fhéachain;
A dúirt mar tharbh go feargach, faobhrach:
"A chrústa mhallaithe, a chaile 's a mhéirligh,
Is dána thugairse duine i gcruith dhaonna 175
In áit ná tigeann aon sciolla den chré ar bith;
Dá mb'fhiú liom mursantacht cumais do dhéanamh
Do rúiscfinn tusa is do ghiolla mar aon leat!"
"Fóill, a churaidh," ar an mhiochardha mhaorga,
"Tóg do chuthach is glac iomacur réitigh; 180
Duine gan bhuairt do fuair mé i ngéarbhroid
De chineachaibh uabhair is d'uaislibh Éireann."
Do rug an macámh ar bharr mo mhéara
'S do rinne sé gáire os árd is béiceach;
Le fuaim a ghutha do chritheadh na spéartha 185
Go gcuala an chruinne é is chuir ifreann géim as!

Téam thar sruthán sa churrachán chaol dubh
'S déanann an t-aithghearr chuig cnocán beag
aerach
Go rángamair eanaí is geataí gan aon ghlas,
An áit a mbíodh maistín ag glamaíl gan traochadh 190
Níor bhréag do Virgil adeireadh 'na bhéarsa
Gurab é seo Cerberus theipeadh an réiteach.
'Na chodhladh bhí ar cheartlár an chosáin 's gan fé
sin
Ach soparnach phiseáin 's é ag srannán 's ag
séideadh:
Do rug an fear fóirnirt de phór na hÉireann 195
Go dubh ar a scórnain le fórsa a ghéaga,
Níor ligeadh don mhadra feacadh ná staonadh
Gur ritheamair thairis fí eagla ár ndaethin.
Níor fhanadh linn go barra an chnoic den réim sin,

Mar ar stadamair ag machnamh's ag féachain; 200
Gur amharcas uaim ann slua ar gach taobh díom
Ag tarraingt máguairt 's ag ruagadh a chéile.
Adúirt linn suí go n-inseadh éifeacht
Is cuntas díreach buíne is béasa.

"Féach-se thall uait clann Gadelus," 205
Ar sé, "agus bantracht mhodhail na hÉireann.
An bhfeicir fir ghroí na Traoi 's na Gréige,
Hector 's a chlaíomh ag maíomh a thréithe,
An seanduine Anchises a chríon le léithe,
A mhac lena thaoibh 's a shínsear éachtach? 210
An gcloisir an glór so ag slógh na héigse
Ag seinm a gceolta is spórt is plé acu?
Horace ann ag mealladh shuilt Mhaecenas
'S dá ngearradh san gan lagadh ar bith le géire.
Ovid ina shuí ar bhínse féir ghlais 215
'S a nóta scríofa síos chun Caesar,
Juvenal 's a phionn idir a mhéara
Is domblas mar dhubh aige is géirnimh:
Aodh Buí Mac Cruitín as Éirinn
'S é ag filíocht go goib-bhinn i nGaeilge – 220
A bprionsa san go ceannsa i suilt dá mbréagadh,
Fonn a ghoib go dtabharfadh duine ón éag leis!
Atáid ansúd, och! trúip na Féinne
Go hárracht, lúdrach, lúbach, léimneach.
Och! a Fhinn Mhic Chumhaill, a chionn na
Féinne, 225
Dá mbeinnse is tú 'nár ndúthaigh ghaolmhair,
Do thabharfaimis abhaile an faraire Séarlas,
Bheadh cabhair dó in Albain nó mealladh mé, 's in
Éirinn.

Machnaighse Liútar d'iompaigh an téarma
'S Calvin ina gcrústa ag cúbhradh méithris; 230
An t-ochtú Hannraí 's a bhainríon bhréagach
Crochta i mbrannraí le slabhraí daora.
Iad so atá scaoilte is chír gan aon ghlas
Béarfar arís go ríocht Mhic Dé isteach!
Imighse abhaile," ar an faraire tréanmhar, 235
"A dhuine seo thagann mar theachtaire as Éirinn:
Is fada bheidh síolra mhíntais Shéamais
Fí cheannas ina rí ag díonadh bhur ngaolta,
Go n-éirí plannda de sheann-tsliocht Éibhir
A dhéanfas conncas i ngeall ar éigean, 240
A bhainfeas an choróin de Sheoirse an éithigh
Is leanfa go fóill de phór Mhilésius.
Seachainse an t-olc do loit síol Éabha,
Gaibh paidir is troscadh is cros Mhic Dé chugat.
Bí déirceach carthannach, ar lasadh le daonnacht, 245
Is réim i bhflaitheas do gheabhair más féidir.
Rachadsa ar siúl, tá liú agus glao orm,
An aicme seo Liútair bhrúdar m'ae ionam:
Do mhairbh an Francach an domhan 's an saol
díobh
'S caithfeadsa a n-iompar anonn don taobh so." 250
Go rófhada sceinn óm radharc den léim sin
Gur thóg Aoibheall íogair léi mé.
Thángamair annso aníos i gcoiníoll nach léir liom
Mar sáitear coinín as poillín le spéice.
Gan stad, ón smúit do mhúscail mé annsan, 255
Mo leaba fúm, mo thrúnc is m'éadach.
Is amhlaidh a bhraitheas mé tarsna gan aon phreab
'S an long ag tarraingt ar Shasana ar foiréigean.
'S é chráigh mo chroí nuair smaoinigh mé annsan

Gach gá ar ghabhas tríd gur thaibhreamh bréige é! 260
Níobh fhada gur labhair an long, "*A sail, a sail,*
The hammocks all down, odzouns she'll take us!"
Frigate bheag Fhrancach lom mhear ghléasta
Chuir sinn i bponc fí scannradh ár ndaethin.
Caitheann sí urchar fí imeall ár n-éadain 265
'S a daichead glan-ghunna dá ligean gach féile,
Go mb'éigean dúinn casadh chomh tapa 's dob
fhéidir
'S pé againn ba mheata chun reatha bheith fé dhe.
Mar a bheadh cúrsa cú agus girrfhéidh aici
Dá chasadh i ngach ponnc 's an cúpla ar saothar 270
Go gcaithfeadh sí stad le neart bheith traochta
Ba mar sin ár gcath-na teacht ar éigean.
Do marbhadh fiche d'ár bhfoirinn san scléip sin,
Ní áirmhim tuilleadh do milleadh bhí créachtach.
Do chailleamair triúr i dtús an lae ghil, 275
Bhí gearradh agus brú ar chúig fhear déag díobh,
Chuaigh urchar i ndailtín an chaptaoin 's níor léan
liom,
Do ghoid sé mo chaipín is níor dhanaoid leis maol
mé.

Rángamair an Pasáiste go batrálta tréithlag
'S thángas-sa go Port Láirge ar cosanáirde im
aonar. 280
Ar loing fad a mhairfead ní rachad má fhéadaim
Mura raghainn le bata nó ceangailte ar théada.
Mar bharra ar gach ní, le Críost bíodh buíochas,
A Chara bhí 'om dhíon, a Rí ná tréig sinn,
Tóg-se t'fhearg dínn, neartaigh is saor sinn, 285
Fóir ar ár n-anam – sin agaibh mo scéalta.

Wedded Bliss

(two extracts from THE MIDNIGHT COURT)

The Poet: Apart from those Irish poets of all centuries up to the present whose identities are totally lost under the label "anonymous," Brian Merriman is the most enigmatic. There is even some dispute about his forebears, whether he was of native Irish or English planter descent. He was born in County Clare some time around the middle of the eighteenth century. He had a small farm, and also kept a school, at Feakle, about twenty miles east of Ennis. It is recorded that he was awarded two prizes by the Dublin Society in 1797, not for poetry, but for the excellence of his flax! Apart from *The Midnight Court*, only two short poems of his are extant. Although his poem, composed around 1780, was popular with Irish scholars and common folk alike, repercussions from other quarters may have been the cause of his later moving with his family to Limerick City where he set up a school. His death in 1805 was reported in newspapers in Ennis, Limerick and Dublin, but he was described only as "a teacher of Mathematics, etc."

The Poem: *The Midnight Court* is undoubtedly the best known of all Irish poems, but unfortunately to most of its readers not in the original Irish but at second hand, in one of the many English translations which have followed on the first, made shortly after Merriman's death by Denis Woulfe of Sixmilebridge in County Clare, a scribe and poet who may actually have known the author. The fact that its vocabulary is the most wideranging and difficult of modern Irish poems has not deterred even those translators whose knowledge of Irish is sparse and who have themselves never written a line of Irish. Inevitably it has also been mangled into several English stage adaptations and at least one lamentable television version in Irish for RTÉ. Even in translation, the poem is usually read for the wrong reasons. The original Irish poem was freely copied, either by fellow-poets or by professional scribes for scholarly collectors – some one hundred mss. have survived – and even memorised by so-called illiterate peasants in County Clare and elsewhere, but as soon as the English version published by Frank O'Connor came to the attention of the Censorship Board which was one of the products of Irish political freedom in 1922, the poem was condemned as lewd and obscene. This would surely have amazed Merriman and his original audience. In fact, the poem is a comprehensive indictment of many of the social and political evils of the period. In the real licentiousness of the modern media, the poem is still habitually labelled bawdy because of passages like those I have translated, which are certainly explicit and comic, but nevertheless are in essence part of the several bitter pills which Merriman has so cleverly coated with the sugar of comedy that the whole purport and purpose of the poem is often overlooked.

WEDDED BLISS

(two extracts from The Midnight Court)

I

The Old Man's Complaint

[Lines 357 – 362]

There then sprang up, all fussy and fierce,
A scruffy old fellow with venomous leer,
His limbs all trembling, puffing hard,
His bony frame with anger barbed. 360
A pitiful sight to the court he seemed,
Like a spectre, then I heard him speak:

[Lines 473 – 530]

"Consider a man who was free as the air
Getting tied till his death 'neath this yoke severe,
To be troubled by jealousy and foolish behaviour 475
Believe me, this lesson was dearly paid for!
'Tis well known all around how I lived my life
For many a year devoid of strife,
A sociable, vigorous, well-to-do man
With a well-furnished house and a welcoming
hand. 480
I had friends in high places, the law on my side,
Influential, a man in whom all might confide.
My speech was of substance and sound effect,
My good sense apparent in land and wealth.
I was peaceful in mind and of fair intent 485
Till a woman robbed me of health and strength.
Attractive and slender and healthy was she,
Well shaped in all parts, a beauty to see,

Her hair flowing full, all waving and bright,
Her features sparkling in morning's light. 490
So virginal seeming, so full of fun,
Inviting kisses from everyone.
Bereft of reason, I shook with desire,
From head to toe with love on fire.
'Tis clear now this was retribution 495
As cruel and sudden as execution
By heaven decreed for sins unwept
That trapped me in that female's net.
The clergy neatly tied the knot
That yoked our lives and future lot, 500
Unstintingly I paid all cost
That by such silly ways is lost.
But fair is fair, on me no blame,
I stopped the rabble's rowdy game
And scattered the beggars, the clerk was pleased, 505
The priest – perhaps with cause? – at ease.
Torches were lit, the neighbours assembled,
Tables were loaded with dishes well-blended,
A clatter of music, the drink flowed free
In a wedding as splendid as ever could be. 510
What a pity that I didn't choke on my food
The night I was christened or before I could
Lie on a bed with a lady fair
Who drove me half-crazy and gave me grey hair.
From old and young I would hear the tale
How she sported and frolicked and called for ale
In the sort of shebeen where roughs used to mingle
And was a soft lay for them, married or single.
Her name and fame were long in crumbling,
'Twas long e'er I'd credit whispers or mumbling.

Others who heard of her carry-on feared
I'd run wild in my pelt and soon disappear.
Still I held out, as blind as a bat,
Every tale that was told I dismissed as trash,
A joke, or the ravings of some poltroon
Till the rumours were certified by her womb.
No more was it nonsense or idle chatter
Or the gossip of women who love to natter
But her action that spoke and for doubt left no room
When she gave me a son that came far too soon . . .

II
Counsel for Defence
[Lines 645 – 756]

The damsel having heard him out 645
Now leapt to her feet and began to shout,
Her patience ended, eyes ablaze,
Her threatening anger rose in waves:

"By Crag's high crown, but that I see
Your shape, and hear your silly speech, 650
And owe this gathering due respect,
I'd tear your head from your scraggy neck.
Below the table I'd knock you flat
And beat you fearfully after that.
I'd quickly sever your life's thin halter 655
And send your soul to Acheron's water.
To answer you I shall not stoop,
You skinny, creeping nincompoop,
But I'll tell this court the story true
Of that lovely lady lost on you. 660
Impoverished and weak, her state was sad,

Comfortless, not even properly clad,
Tired of her life, without hearth or home,
From pillar to post she drifted alone.
No place to rest by day or night, 665
On crusts from inferiors forced to bite.
A change of life this wretch then promised,
All homely comforts he'd lavish on her,
Secure and clean, fine cows to keep,
A feather-bed for slumber deep. 670
A cosy hearth with turf unstinted,
Well-sodded walls no breeze e'er dinted,
Shelter secure from wind and weather,
Wool and flax to spin without measure.
Everyone knew, this worm knew well, 675
That it wasn't affection or love's bright spell
Brought such a beauty so to be tied
But poverty and hunger unsatisfied.
Her pleasure at night now became her doom,
A labour of trouble, distress and gloom, 680
Under limbs like lead and shoulders thin
And bony knees that froze her skin.
Withered old legs dried up by the fire
And a carcass decrepit more dead than alive.
Is there any fair lady who wouldn't go grey 685
If she found herself bound 'neath that heap to stay,
That twice in one year never bothered to find
Was she fish, was she flesh, or of boyish kind,
But shrivelled and cold beside her stretched,
A wrinkled, morose, unrousable wretch? 690
Oh, how she longed for a nightly rumble,
As hot as hell she'd gladly tumble,
Surely you cannot feel *she* was to blame

Or think her reluctant to play love's game?
So handsome and healthy, so fond and refined, 695
Assuredly hers was a well-formed mind.
She'd never complain if it went the night long,
She could give as she got, no matter how strong.
His faintest efforts she'd never despise
But lay on her back and closed her eyes. 700
Nor would she jerk in sulking mood
Or scrape or scratch him as a cat would,
But lay all flowing smooth and slim,
Side by side, her arm around him.
With stories she tried to coax his passion, 705
Her mouth on his, her fingers fastening,
Around him curled her leg would be,
She'd stroke her brush from waist to knee,
The bedclothes all snatch from his rump,
Toying in play with that joyless lump. 710
In vain she tickled and rubbed and squeezed,
With nail, with elbow, even with heel,
A shame to tell how she spent the night
Cuddling that heap, then lying aside
With cramping arms, the sheets bedraggled, 715
Her limbs all trembling, teeth that chattered,
No wink of sleep till dawn of day,
Tossing and moaning, there she lay.

So well may this wretch about women speak,
With his impotent loins and old bones so weak. 720
If this gentle beauty, sorely in need,
Did an illicit act, then I favour the deed.
Will the fox on the mountain, the fish in the sea,
The high-soaring eagle or herds of wild deer

Stay fasting like fools for a year or a day 725
While everywhere offered to take what they may?
Can you imagine an insect or beast
On bare earth or heather choosing to feast
Or nibbling at hedges when there, all around,
Sweet plants and green grass in plenty are found? 730
Come, tell us at once, you mean-souled weasel,
Answer me, let us hear good reason:
Does it lessen your share when you need a bite
That feeding others was her delight?
Does it weaken a grove or lay the land bare 735
If millions have passed in a season there?
Are you such a dolt, you feeble old weed,
As to fear there will not be enough for your need?
Or maybe you're so far gone as to cry
That the Shannon itself could be drunk dry? 740
That the ebbing sea with its tidal span
And the ocean deep could be drained with a can?
You'd need to check your silly notions
And bandage your head to halt its dotage.
Take care you do not fall into fits 745
For fear how women bestow their gifts.
If she spent the whole day giving freely to all
She'd have more than enough to answer your call.
Jealousy, alas! one could well understand
In an agile, vigorous, virile man, 750
Lusty and lively, constant in pleasuring,
Giving and taking without any measuring,
Or in some dashing lad, some competent guest,
Some flailer unfailing forever at best,
But not in this withered and worn old fool, 755
A worker weak with a useless tool.

SONAS AN PHÓSTA

(dhá shliocht as Cúirt an Mheán-Oíche)

I

Gearán an tSeanduine

[Línte 357 – 362]

Preabann anuas go fuadrach fíochmhar
Seanduine suarach is fuadach nimhe fé,
A bhaill ar luascadh is luais anáile air,
Draighean is duais ar fuaid a chnámha. 360
Ba dhearóil an radharc go deimhin don chúirt é,
Ar bord 'na thaibhse im eisteacht dúirt sé:

[Línte 473 – 530]

"Breathain gur baol don té tá scaoilte
Ceangal go héag fá thaobh don chuing seo,
I sealbh gach saoth is éad dá shuaitheadh, 475
In aisce, mo léan, mo léann ní bhfuair mé.
Is feasach don taobh seo 'on tsaol mar bhí mé
Sealad dom réim 's dom laethaibh roimhe seo,
Leitheadach láidir lán do shaibhreas,
Éisteas le fáil is fáilte im theaghlach, 480
Caraid i gcúirt is cúnamh dlí agam,
Ceannas is clú agus comhar na saoithe,
Tathag im chaint is suim is éifeacht,
Talamh is maoin ag suíomh mo chéille,
M'aigne síoch is m'intinn sásta, 485
Gur chailleas le mnaoi mo bhrí is mo shláinte.
Ba thaithneamhach leabhair an crobhaire mná í,
Bhí seasamh is com is cabhail is cnámha aici
Casadh 'na cúl go búclach trilseach,
Lasadh 'na gnúis go lonrach soilseach, 490

Cuma na hóighe uirthi is só ina gáire
Is cuireadh ina cló chum póige is fáilte.
Ach creathas le fonn gan chonn gan chairde
Ó bhaitheas go bonn go tabhartha i ngrá dhi.
Is dearbh gan dabhta ar domhan gur díoltas 495
Danartha donn, dom thabhairt ar m'aimhleas
D'fhearthain go trom, ar bhonn mo ghníomhartha,
Ó fhlaitheas le fonn, do lom 'na líon mé.
Do snamanadh suíte snaidhm na cléire
Is ceangladh sinn i gcuing re chéile, 500
Ghlanas gan chinnteacht suim gach éilimh
Bhaineas le baois gan ghaois an lae sin.
Cothrom go leor níor chóir mé cháineadh,
Stopas an gleo bhí ag cóip na sráide,
Bacaigh go léir, bhí an cléireach sásta, 505
An sagart ró-bhaoch is b'fhéidir fáth leis.
Lasamair toirse is comharsain cruinn ann
Is leagadh ar bordaibh mórchuid bídh chúinn,
Clagarnach ceoil is ól gan choimse
Is chaitheadar cóisir mhórtach mhaíteach. 510
Mo dhíth gan easpa nár tachtadh le bia mé
An oíche baisteadh nó as sin gur iarr mé
Síneadh ar leabain le ainnir do liath mé
Is scaoil le gealaigh gan charaid gan chiall mé.
Is é tásc do gheobhainn ag óg 's ag aosta 515
Gur breallán spóirt ag ól 's ag glaoch í
I mbotháin ósta is boird dá bpléascadh,
Ar lár 'na lóiste ag pósta is aonta.
B'fhada dhá mheilt a teist 's a tuairisc,
B'fhada gur chreid mé a bheag ná a mhuar dhe, 520
B'eaglach le gach beirt dá gcuala é
Go rachainn im pheilt im gheilt gan tuairisc.

Fós ní ghéillfinn, caoch mar bhí mé,
Do ghlór gan éifeacht éinne mhaígh é,
Ach magadh nó greim gan feidhm gan chéill 525
Gur aithris a broinn dom deimhin gach scéil.
Níor chúrsaí leamhais ná durdam bréige é,
Dúirt bean liom go ndúradh léithi é,
Ach labhair an bheart i gceart 's in éifeacht –
Bhronn sí mac i bhfad roimh ré orm. 530

I

AN CHÚIS DÁ COSAINT

[Línte 645 – 756]

Tar éis bheith tamall don ainnir ag éisteacht 645
Léim 'na seasamh go tapa gan foighne,
Labhair sí leis agus leise 'na súile
Is rabhartaí feirge feille aici fúthu.

"Dar coróin na Carraige marach le géilleadh
Dhod chló dhod ainnise is d'easnamh do chéille 650
Is d'am na hurraime 'on chuideachta shéimh seo
An ceann lem ingin do sciobfainn dod chaolscrog.
Do leagfainn anuas do thuairt fán mbord tú
Is b'fhada le lua gach cuaird dá ngeobhainn ort,
Stróicfinn sreangaibh do bheatha le fonn ceart 655
Is sheolfainn t'anam go Acheron tonntach.
Ní fiú liom freagra freastail do thabhairt ort,
A shnamhaire fhleascaigh nach aithis do labhartha,
Ach neosad feasta do mhaithibh na cúirte
An nós ar cailleadh an ainnir nárbh fhiú thu. 660

Do bhí sí lag gan ba gan puntaibh,

Bhí sí i bhfad gan teas gan clúdach,
Cortha dá saol ar strae dhá seoladh
Ó phosta go piléar gan gaol gan cóngas,
Gan scíth gan spás do lá ná dh'oíche 665
Ag stríocadh an aráin ó mhná nár chuí léi.
Do gheall an fear seo dreas socúil di,
Gheall an spreas di teas is clúide,
Cothrom glan is ba le crú dhi
Is codladh fada ar leabain chlúimh di, 670
Teallaí teo agus móin a daoithin
Is ballaí fód gan lóithne gaoithe,
Fothain is díon ón sín is ón spéir di
Is olann is líon le sníomh chun éadaigh.
Do b'fheasach dhon tsaol 's don phéist seo
láithreach 675
Nách taitneamh ná téamh aon phioc grá dho
Cheangail an péarla maorga mná so,
Ach easnamh go léir, ba déirc léi an tsástacht.
Ba dubhach an fuadar suairceas oíche,
Smúit is ualach, duais is líonadh, 680
Lúithní lua agus guaille caola
Is glúine crua chomh fuar le oighre,
Cosa feoite dóite ón ngríosaigh
Is colann bhreoite dhreoite chríonna.
An bhfuil stuaire beo ná feofadh liath 685
Ag cuail dá shórt bheith pósta riamh
Nár chuartaigh fós fá dhó le bliain
Cé buachaill óg í, feoil nó iasc,
'S an feoiteach fuar seo suas léi sínte
Dreoite duairc, gan bhua gan bhíogadh? 690
Óch, cár mhuar dhi bualadh bríomhar
Ar nós an diabhail de uair gach oíche.

Ní dóch go dtuigir gurb ise ba chiontach
Ná fós go gclisfeadh ar laige le tamhandacht,
An maighre mascalach carthanach ciúintais, 695
Is deimhin go bhfeaca sí a mhalairt do mhúineadh.
Ní labharfadh focal dá mb'obair an oíche
Is thabharfadh cothrom do stollaire bríomhar,
Go brách ar siúl níor dhiúltaigh riamh é
Ar chnáimh a cúil 's a súilibh iata. 700
Ní thabharfadh preab le stailc mhíchuíosach,
Fobha mar chat nó sraic nó scríob air,
Ach í go léir 'na slaod chomh sínte
Taobh ar thaobh 's a géag 'na thimpeall,
Ó scéal go scéal ag bréagadh a smaointe, 705
Béal ar bhéal 's ag méaracht síos air.
Is minic do chuir sí a cos dtaobh anonn de
Is chuimil a *brush* ó chrios go glún de,
Sciobadh an phluid 's an chuilt dá ghúnga
Ag spriongar 's ag sult le moirt gan subhachas. 710
Níor chabhair di cigilt ná cuimilt ná fáscadh,
Fobha dá hingin, dá huillinn ná a sála,
Is nár dom aithris mar chaitheadh sí an oíche
Ag fáscadh an chnaiste 's ag searradh 's ag
síneadh,
Ag feacadh na ngéag 's an t-éadach fúithi, 715
A ballaibh go léir 's a déid ar lúthchrith,
Go loinnir an lae gan néall do dhubhadh uirthi
Ag imirt ó thaobh go taobh 's ag únfairt.

Nach foras don lobhar so labhairt ar mhná
Is gan fuinneamh 'na chom ná cabhair 'na
chnámha 720
Má d'imigh an mhodhamhail bhí trom 'ná ghá

Is gur deineadh an fhoghail seo, gabhaimse a páirt.
An bhfuil sionnach ar sliabh ná iasc i dtráigh
Ná fiolar le fiach ná fiaigh le fán
Comh fada gan chiall le bliain ná lá 725
Do chaitheamh gan bia 's a bhfiach le fáil?
An aithnid díbh féin sa tsaol so cáil
An t-ainmhí claon ná an féithid fáin
Do phiocfadh an chré ná an fraoch ná an fál
Is fiorthann go slaodach is féar le fáil? 730
Aithris gan mhoill, a chladhaire chráite,
Freagair mé, faighimse feidhm id ráite:
Ca bhfuil do dhíth ag suí chum béile
Ar caitheadh le mí aici i dtíos na féile?
An laigede an chúil nó an lúide an láithreach 735
Fiche milliún má shiúil le ráithe ann?
Mairg id cheann, a sheandaigh thamhanda,
An eagal leat ganntan am do dhúla?
An dóch, a ghliogaire buile, gur baol leat
Ól na Sionainne tirim nó a taoscadh, 740
Trá na farraige is tarraingt an tsáile
Is clár na mara do scaipeadh le scála?
Breathain in am ar leamhas do smaointe
Is ceangail do cheann le banda thimpeall,
Seachain i dtráth, ná fág do chiall 745
Le eagla mná bheith fáilteach fial.
Dá gcaitheadh sí an lá le cách dá riar
Bheadh tuilleadh is do sháithse ar fáil 'na ndiaidh.
Mo chumha, mo chrá, ba bhreá sin éad
Ar lúbaire láidir lánmhear léadmhar, 750
Shantach sháitheach shásta sheasmhach,
Ramsach ráflach rábach rabairneach,
Lascaire luaimneach, cuartóir coimseach,

Balcaire buan nó buailteoir bríomhar,
Ach seanduine seanda cranda créimeach, 755
Feamaire fann is feam gan féile.

Lament For A Bailiff

The Poet: Unlike the poets of Munster in the 18th Century, Riocard Bairéad, born in County Mayo around the year 1729, did not have the advantage of a court or school of fellow-poets to stimulate his output. Although folklore tells of his being a renowned scholar and schoolmaster, who spent some time in prison for his activites during the brief and tentative effort of the French Revolution to extend its helping hand to the Irish rebels of 1798, only a handful of his poems have survived orally to be written down by later collectors. This poem, in which he ironically laments the death of an extortionate bailiff – naming some local people who had obviously special cause to rejoice – and a rousing drinking song, *Preab san Ól*, which is still popular, are the two pieces by which he is best known.

The Poem: The Irish world *cóir*, which the poet uses as a mockingly affectionate substitute for the bailiff's surname, has a variety of meanings, such as *just, honest, decent, righteous, fair, proper.* Satires on dead landlords or their even more merciless bailiffs are understandably frequent in Irish, but the comic irony of this piece is perhaps more effective than some of the forthright maledictory abuse heaped on the tombs of others of the species, such as the sonorous satire, *Faoi Lár na Lice Seo*, on the death of a land-agent named Dawson in Co. Tipperary (who is not named in the poem, of course). Attributed to the great Munster poet, Aogán Ó Rathaille (1675-1728), that famous satire begins with a line which sets the hammer-blow tone of the whole:

"Faoi lár na lice seo curtha tá an ollaphiast ramhar . . ."

(Under this flagstone buried is the corpulent monster . . .)

The final stanza of the present piece links it to the carefree author of the aforementioned drinking-song, obviously a man who was not much concerned with the fate of his verses so long as they gave entertainment to the people of his own community for whom they were composed.

LAMENT FOR A BAILIFF

Isn't this painful news we've been hearing,
That causes us heartbreak and woe,
It spreads outward from Creggan-a-Leena
All the way till it reaches Faulmore.
The likes of such wailing and weeping
Never heard in this country before,
And no wonder, since we're all a-keening
The death, alas! of Fair Owen.

There was none but regarded him fondly,
He was cherished by all, young and old,
The rich and the poor all adored him

Because of his heart's goodly store.
In all quarters, to all and sundry,
He scattered his pieces of gold,
Nor scorned with the poorest of people
A jar from the shebeen to hold.

Hear Anthony Gavin lamenting!
And John Boyle will soon be at death's door,
Since they heard their good friend has departed,
Their hearts are near breaking with woe.
There ne'er fell in the battle's hard struggle,
To be laid 'neath the sod or the stone,
Any man to that pair could be dearer
Than this harmless poor fellow, Fair Owen.

At gathering the rent he was powerful,
A month or two he'd let it go
Till the cow for the fair was in order
Or the cloth from the loom could be sold.
Old Seamus McCreevy beseeches
Our heavenly Lord on his throne:
The same treatment he dealt to our people
Let Christ hand out now to Fair Owen.

Write a one and a seven behind it,
Put two eights after that in a row,
When his final farewell was recited,
Not a geeks after that did he blow.
Now we know that it's solemnly chronicled,
All life to the dark earth must go,
So as long as we're here in this world
We might as well drink a drop more!

CAOINEADH AR BHÁILLE

Nach é seo an scéal deacrach sa tír seo,
In anacair chroí agus bróin,
Ó fhágas sé Creagán a' Líne
Go dté sé go dtí an Fál Mór.
A leithéid de screadadh 's de chaoineadh
Níor cluineadh sa tír seo fós,
Gidh níl againn aon ionadh
Ó cailleadh, faraoir! Eoghan Cóir.

Bhí gnaoi agus gean ag gach n-aon air,
An seanduine críon is an t-óg,
Bhí an saibhir is an daibhir i ngrá leis
Mar gheall ar a chroí maith mór.
Le togha 's le rogha na tíre
Do chaitheadh sé píosaí óir,
'S le daoine bocht' eile níor spíd leis
Buidéal ón síbín d'ól.

Tá Antoine Ó Gabháin ag caoineadh
Is ní bheidh Seán Ó Baoill i bhfad beo
Ó cailleadh a gcaraid sa tír seo
'Sé d'fhág a gcroí faoi bhrón.
In anacair catha níor síneadh,
Is é mheasaim, faoi liag ná fód
Aon neach ba mheasa don dís seo
Ná na duine bocht maol Eoghan Cóir.

Ba ró-mhaith ag tógáil an chíos' é,
Ba bheag aige mí nó dhó

Go ndíoltaí an bhó ar an aonach
Nó an giota a bhíodh sa tseol.
'Sé dúirt Séamas Pheadair Mhic Riabhaigh,
Is é ag agairt ar Rí na nDeor,
De réir mar bhí seisean le daoine
Gurab amhlaidh bhéas Críosta dhó.

Aon agus seacht ins an líne
Agus ocht a chur síos faoi dhó
Tráth ghlac seisean cead lena dhaoine
Is níor labhair sé gíog níos mó.
Tá sé go dearfa scríofa
Gur talamh is críoch do gach beo,
Is chomh fada is bheimid sa saol seo
Cá miste dhúinn braon beag d'ól!

Blind Raftery And The Thorn Tree

The Poet: Antoine Ó Reachtabhra was born around the year 1784 in Cill Aodáin near Coillte Mach in County Mayo. His surname later became anglicised as Raftery, the name by which he is now generally known. An attack of smallpox left him blind at the age of nine. He was taught to play the fiddle as a means of saving him from beggary, but he was gifted by nature with a greater talent – he was to become the best-known and most-quoted poet of his own time and long after; even today, most Irish people will react to his name by quoting a few lines from the short autobiographical poem attributed to him, *Mise Raifteirí an File* ("I am Raftery the Poet"). He left his native Mayo in early manhood and spent the rest of his life wandering the roads of east Galway, playing the fiddle "for empty pockets" as the aforementioned poem puts it, composing his poems as he tramped the long roads, and reciting them at the firesides where he was given hospitality by the so-called illiterate peasants whose ability to memorize them was to ensure their survival until they were written down by local teachers and rural scholars, and later in the century by Dr. Douglas Hyde and Lady Gregory, who were among those responsible, in 1900, for the erection of a tombstone over the poet's hitherto unmarked grave in Killineen cemetery near Craughwell in County Galway.

The Poem: In its entirety of ninety-nine four-line stanzas, this is not a comic poem, since it is basically a verse narration of the history of Ireland from mythological times up to the "War of the Two Kings" as the Jacobite or Williamite war of 1689-91 is known in Irish. The comic element is in the long prologue in which the blind poet shows his originality and more than a touch of pure genius by preparing us for the story of Ireland – as told by a very ancient and eloquent thorn tree! It is this section which I have translated. The rest of the poem contains some deft touches, like the line referring to the cowardly King James who fled from the Boyne and from Ireland, leaving the Irish to continue the struggle to regain his throne from his son-in-law, William of Orange: "Ach Séamas a' chaca, mallacht Dé dhó . . . " ("But Shamus the shite, the curse o' God on him . . ."). Inevitably, however, much of it is a trite folk retelling of the plain facts of history.

BLIND RAFTERY AND THE THORN TREE

One August day I chanced to be
Near Headford in the pouring rain,
I moved aside, quite sensibly,
Shelter near hedge or bush to gain.

All I could find, beside a gap,
Was a battered crooked old thorn tree
On the side of a ditch and sloping down;
Under that was still a wet place to be.

From every quarter the rain was pelting,
From east and west to slant it seemed,
So bad it was I can hardly tell you,
As if a great sieve were winnowing seed.

Fierce and furious the rain came storming,
Swift as arrows or a full mill-race,
Then sleet came on, the fields were drowning,
And poor me shelterless in that place!

For an hour and a quarter the rain poured down
In drops that many a can would o'erflow,
Every mill in the province, for meal or flour,
In the open fields it would keep on the go.

I began to think, and who could blame me?
That my end was near and my time decreed,
That this was a deluge to drown all nations,
And my life could show only evil deeds.

From childhood on, my sins were many,
My language foul, no thought of grace,
From Sunday Mass I would often tarry,
Nor at Christmas or Easter would I confess.

The Ten Commandments I broke regardless,
My neighbour's woe just made me laugh,
In gaming, drinking, in every madness
That came my way I played my part.

Long tho' the lease, there comes the reckoning,
My summons written and duly drawn,
But my web unwoven, the weft still wanting,
And tomorrow my case due to be called.

Then going to that place where welcome waits
For rich and poor on equal terms,
The good or evil of all your days
Clear on your forehead is affirmed.

Devoutly then I thus repented:
"O God in heaven, source of all graces,
Who gives light to moon and bloom to deserts,
Who rules the sea, sets sun a-blazing,

Makes trees bear fruit, ships safe arrive,
Brought Israelites from their foes' harsh heel,
Took Enoch and Elias to Paradise,
Made wine from water at your Mother's heed,

Look down from heaven on Patrick's Island
As on crucified thief you turned your face,
You did all the wonders I have recited,
Now save me and all of Adam's race."

And then the thought came to my mind
Of what in the Bible is set down,
God's promise that while rainbow shines
The earth in a deluge will never drown.

Soon after that the rain eased off,
The sun shone bright, a fresh wind blew;
Battered and drenched I then moved on,
To John's house came and a welcome true.

Many a quart of water he wrung
From my old cape and all I wore,
On a nail my dripping hat he hung,
On a soft bed stretched my carcase sore.

I soon recovered and rose restored,
My fiddle made music for sport and dance,
We had such a night as never before
And all enjoyed good fortune's chance.

Next day my steps I slow retraced,
Crossed by the ford and knew the ground,
These words sharply I then addressed
To that same old tree where I nearly drowned:

"Ugly old Thorn Tree, curses on you!
May you never again bear fruit or flower!
Great Oscar's flailing blows shower on you
And blacksmith's hammer break you down!

To meet with you was my bad luck,
Poor shelter found I at your side,
No drop that hit your twisted trunk
But you poured on me from your wrinkled hide."

TREE

"If you come, poet, a duel demanding,
I stand before you here on guard,
An ancient I, long ages standing,
Approach no nearer with your sword.

If you stood near me in my prime
You'd shelter safe from wind and rain,
'Twas the east wind wore me down with time
And left me bent with branches bare."

RAFTERY

"Fair Thorn Tree, of great renown,
God grant that flower and fruit you'll bear,
Apples, pears, plums and damsons shower!
Your great age now I'd gladly hear."

TREE

"One thousand and one hundred years
Before the Ark was built I grew,
Since then I have been standing here
And many's the tale I have for you . . ."

RAIFTEIRÍ DALL AGUS AN SCEACH

Tráth faoi Lúnas' ba dhomhsa tharla
Ar bhord Áth Cinn 's é go mór ag báisteach,
Do dhruid mé ar leataoibh is ní gan ábhar
Go bhfaighinn claí nó tom do dhéanfadh scáth
dhom.

Ní bhfuair mé ann i leataoibh bearnan
Ach sean-sceach chaite, chraite, chráite,
Ar thaobh an chlaí is a haghaidh le fána:
Dhruid mé fúithi 's ba fhliuch an áit dom.

Bhí an fhearthainn go dian ag teacht as gach
cearda,
Anoir is aniar is anuas le fána,
A samhail ní fhéadfainn thabhairt duit
láithreach
Ach roithleán lán bheadh ag criathrú ráibe.

Go feargach, fraochmhar, stoirmiúil, rágach,
Mar bheadh saigheada ar luas nó aghaidh ar rása
Bhí an chascairt ag tíocht 's na tíortha báite,
'S nár mise an díol trua i gcruas gan scáth ar bith!

Uair agus ceathrú do bhí sé ag báisteach,
'S ní raibh braon nach gcuirfeadh maol ar
chárta,
Níl muileann sa chúige plúir nó ráibe
Nach gcuirfeadh sé ar siúl i lár na mbánta.

Rinne mé smaointe, ní nár náir dhom,
Nárbh fhada mo shaol 's mbá ghearr mo
chairde,
Go dtiocfadh an díle 's go mbeadh daoine báite
'S go mba olc an obair bhí i ndiaidh mo
láimhe.

Bheith ag déanamh peaca dhom ó bhí mé 'mo
pháiste,
Ag lua mionnaí móra 's ag gearradh na ngrása,
Dul chun Aifrinn ní iarrfainn trácht air
Nó faoistin Nollag a fháil nó Cásca.

Na Deich nAitheanta a bhriseadh ní ghnínn cás
de,
Faoi bhris mo chomharsa ar ndóigh ghnínn
gáire,
Gach imirt, gach ól, gach aon phléaráca
Dá dtagadh trasna orm, bhíodh mo lámh ann.

Da fhaid é an t-am tig an cáirde
Go mbeidh an *summons* ann scríofa
tarraingthe,
Tá an uige in easnamh 's an t-inneach gan fáil
air
Agus triail mo chúise ar siúl amárach.

Bheith ag dul san áit nach mbíonn aon fháilte ann
Roimh shaibhir thar bhocht ach de réir a
gcáilíocht,
An t-olc is an mhaith ó bhí tú id' pháiste
Thíos le léamh ar t'éadan tarraingthe.

Ar aithrí smaoiníos mar so go cráifeach:
'A Dhia tá thuas is ghníos na grása,
Thug solas ar ghealaigh is fás ar fhásach,
A stiúraíos an mhuir 's do chuir grian in airde,

"Thug toradh ar chrainn agus longa ó
bháitheadh,
Thug na hIsraelítigh ó chosaibh a námhad,
Thug Enoc is Elias go gáirdín Phárrthais,
'S rinne fíon den uisce le toil do Mháthar,

"Féach anuas ar Oileán Phádraig
Mar d'fhéach tú ar an ngadaí ar chrann na
Páise,
Rinne tú gach ní dá bhfuil agam ráite:
Tabhair mise saor leat is clann bhocht
Ádhaimh."

Do rinne mé smaointiú arís ar ball air,
Go bhfuil sé san mBíobla scríofa tarraingthe,
Gealladh glan díreach ó Rí na ngrása,
Fad a bhéas stua-cheatha cam nár bhaol dúinn
báitheadh.

Ba ghearr ina dhiaidh sin gur lag an bháisteach,
Grian gur las agus gaoth gur ardaigh,
Gur ghluais mé ar siúl 's mé múchta báite,
Gur tharraing mé tigh Sheáin agus bhí romham
fáilte.

Is iomaí sin cárta uisce d'fháisc sé
As mo sciorta go dtí mo chába,
Chroch sé mo hata suas ar tháirne
Agus chuir sé 'mo chodladh mé ar leaba
bhláfar.

Níorbh fhada go bhfacthas 'mo shuí arís mé
Ag cur mire ar cheol, spórt agus siamsa,
'S ar ndóigh le bród is fós le haoibhneas
Do ghlacamar faill is meidhir na hoíche.

Ar n-iompó thart dom, lá arna mhárach,
Siolla beag uaim le ciúmhais na hátha,
Siúd mar a dúirt mé ar theacht i láthair
Na sean-sceiche céanna faoina raibh mé báite:

"A shean-sceachán ghránna, fuagraim gráin
ort!
Ná raibh a-choíche snua ná bláth ort!
Faoi shúiste Oscair go bhfaighe tú do chárnadh,
Dod' bhrú is dod' bhriseadh ag ord mór
ceártan.

"Dob olc an áit dom teacht i ndáil leat
Ná druidim fút ag iarraidh scáith ort,
Níl braon dár bhuail faoi do cham-stoc gránna
Nár scaoil tú anuas orm le ciúmhais do mhása."

AN SCEACH

Más file tusa tá ag iarraidh sásaimh
Tá mise anseo romhat ar garda,
Is seanóir mé atá i bhfad san áit seo
'S ná tar níos gaire dhom le do chlaíomh
tarraingthe.

Nuair a bhí mise óg dá mbeifeá i ndáil liom
Ba fhogas duit díon ó ghaoith 's ó bháisteach,
'Sí an ghaoth aniar d'fhág m'aghaidh le fána
'S do shiosc mé síos ó bharr go sála."

RAIFTEIRÍ

"A sceacháin mhaiseach, shochlach, bhláfar,
Snua 'gus snas ort ó Rí na ngrása,
Úlla, piorraí, plumaí is bláistí,
Agus cuir dom síos aois do dháta."

AN SCEACH

Céad agus míle roimh am na hÁirce
Tús agus cruthú m'aois is mo dháta;
Tá mé ó shin im' shuí san áit seo,
'Gus is iomaí scéal a bhféadaim trácht air . . ."

A Malediction On Tobacco

The Poet: His name is not known, and his poem being in the older form might lead one to believe that he was a medieval poet; but the subject of his poem dates him at least after the bardic schools had begun to disintegrate in the early 17th century. He could be a later imitator of the syllabic forms of the classical style – even in modern times some poets (including myself!) have written poems in Irish which imitate the medieval classical forms in adhering to the syllabic line and the complicated rhyme scheme (the latter at least in the vocalic assonance; the complications of the consonantal correspondences which were also *de rigueur* in the classical forms are beyond anyone who did not pursue the rigorous seven year course of training in the bardic schools).

The Poem: Modern health authorities trying to curb or eliminate smoking might find some useful advertising material in the list of evil effects given by the poet, including the unusual one of the loss of sexual desire! The theme is not original or unique: the arguments for and against tobacco began almost with its introduction to Europe. In *The Fairire Queen* (1596) Spenser refers to "divine tobacco" as the equivalent of a panacea, while no less a personage than King James I of England warned against its evil effects (*A Counterblaste to*

Tobacco, 1604). Robert Burton, author of *The Anatomy of Melancholy* (1621) was a man who would be described in Irish as a "*Tadhg an Dá Thaobh*" (Tim-Two-Sides), in English as one who "runs with the hare and hunts with the hounds"; as he puffs his pipe by his own fireside, the learned clergyman says: "Tobacco, divine, rare, superexcellent tobacco, which goes far beyond all their panaceas, potable gold, and philosopher's stones, a sovereign remedy to all diseases." But then, mounting his pulpit, he warns: "But, as it is commonly abused by most men, which take it as tinkers do ale, 'tis a plague, a mischief, a violent purger of goods, lands, health; hellish, devilish and damned tobacco, the ruin and overthrow of body and soul."

A MALEDICTION ON TOBACCO

Away with the stinking tobacco,
In my mouth it will ne'er go again;
By it breath and the teeth are damaged,
The chest harmed in many men.

It robs you of memory and sense,
The legs go bent in their stride,
It sets up a buzz in the head,
Causes pearl to grow on the eye.

Never grew any herb more vile
On the soil of Conn's green land,
It makes silver and gold disappear,
Leaves the heirs with empty hands.

Few of its faults go unshared,
From far lands it came to our isle;
Of this women should well be aware:
In menfolk it weakens desire.

Who would wish a long life to enjoy
Need not find any reason more:
It was Lucifer, master of guile,
First decided that tree to grow.

MALLACHT AR AN TOBAC

Beir uaimse an tobac bréan,
  Ní rachaidh sé i mo bhéal go bráth;
Milleann sé anáil is déad,
  Agus lagann sé clabhrach cáich.

Goideann sé an chuimhne is an chiall,
  Baineann sé an triall den chois,
Fágann sé dursan 'sa gcionn
  Agus tógann sé fionn ar rosc.

'Sí an luibh is measa d'fhás
  Ar chlár Bhanba Choinn;
Spréann sí airgead is ór
  Agus caitheann sí an stór ón gclainn.

Is beag dá lochtaibh gan roinn,
  Tháinig thar toinn is thar lear;
Do mhnáibh dá gcuirfeadh é i suim:
  Cloíonn sí fonn na bhfear.

Gach aon ar mhian a bheith buan
  Ní beag dó mar ghráin is mar chúis
Gurab é Lúsaifer na meang
  Do thionscain an crann ar dtúis.

The New Maestro

The Poet: A native of County Armagh, Art Benaid (or Beinéid, Bennet) was better known as a scholar, scribe and collector of songs and manuscripts than as a poet. Perhaps it was his critical study of poetry and music that developed the sensitive feeling for both which gave rise to this satire, by which he is now represented in the anthologies. On the other hand, he may have been motivated by that envy which is endemic in the artistic temperment.

The Poem: The use of hyperbole, or exaggeration to create an effect, was a favourite device even in the old Celtic sagas and in the stories about Fionn Mac Cumhaill and the Fianna. Indeed, it is a common feature of even colloquial speech in Ireland – where English says "Welcome" the Irish equivalent is "Céad Míle Fáilte." (A hundred thousand welcomes!) An Irish child having collected twenty chestnuts in the Autumn will tell his envious friends that he "got *millions* of them," and there is a story of a drowsy old priest in the confessional who was startled to attention by a young voice piping from the darkness: "Father, I *murdered* my sister six times." Apart from this literary effect, the poem is of some technical interest because, although the lines are in the modern stress metre, the vocalic rhyme-scheme is that of the older syllabic forms. The meaningful Irish place-names naturally lend more of a euphonic effect to the original poem than the anglicised transcriptions can do in an English version – the latter are often totally meaningless in their English forms, as in *Kilkeel* and *Kells*. To an Irish speaker, the name *Eas Aoidh Rua* (The Waterfall of Red Hugh) has even historic connotations; its anglicised corruption, *Assaroe*, is not even a meaningful English word. The same lamentable cultural loss is apparent on most of the bilingual road-signs of Ireland; compare the old Irish name, *Cill*, meaning church, with its phonetic English transcription, *Kill* – and the village so named is in County *Kildare*, in Irish *Cill Dara*, the Church of the Oak Tree. I have refrained from thus maltreating some of the place-names in the poem, giving a general geographic exaggeration instead.

THE NEW MAESTRO

The fish that used to swim in the Boyne
Went harvesting to Donegal
When they heard Hugh O'Donnell begin to
whine
His verses, his new songs to bawl.

The swan changed colour to black as coal,
The fox took cobbling as a trade,
The fly drank dry all Assaroe
On hearing the music this maestro made.

The wren transported in his beak
John's Castle up to Ballymeer,
Then sent the snail the news to break
From the bay of Howth up to Kilkeel.

In Waterford a whistle blew
That sent Armagh to Cashel south,
Kells to County Clare then flew
And hills went on a roundabout.

A trip to Carling Tara took,
And Moate old Derry went to view,
From north to south the country shook
In welcome for the maestro new.

AN tOLLAMH ÚR

D'imigh an t-iasc a bhí sa Bhóinn
A dhéanamh fómhair go Dún na nGall
Tráth chuala siad Aodh Mac Domhnaill
Bheith ag ceartú ceoil is ag cumadh rann.

D'iompaigh an eala ar dhath an ghuail
Is an madra rua ina ghréasaí bróg.
Thriomaigh an mhíoltóg Eas Aoidh Rua
Le neart a lúcháire fá ollamh an cheoil.

Scuab an dreoilín leis ina bhéal
Caisleán Seáin go Baile an Mhaoir,
Agus chuir sé an seilide leis an scéal
Ó Chuan Bhinn Éadair go Cill a' Chaoil.

Séideadh feadóg istigh i bPort Láirge
Agus d'imigh Ard Mhacha go Caiseal
    Mumhan,
D'imigh Ceannanas go Contae an Chláir
Agus Cnoc an Bhráthar go Lios a' Phúc'.

D'imigh Teamhair go sléibhte Cháirlinn'
Agus Móta Gránard go Doire Núis',
D'imigh Cuan na Mara go Baile Uí Bhragáin
'Cur iomad fáilte don ollamh úr.

The Spinning Wheel

The Poet: If the monastic poets refrained from signing their poems because of humility or fear of the abbot, and the poets of the Hidden Ireland of the 18th Century through fear of the English authorities and the landlords, the author of this comically plaintive ditty had much more personal reason for not claiming credit for his artistic work – his future output would probably have been severely curtailed if his wife realized that she was the slovenly woman in question. On the other hand, just as in the case of the leisurely authors of the medieval poems of courtly love, this poet may have been a bachelor composing a song "just for divilment" as we say. In his book, *Enemies of Promise*, the English critic, Cyril Connolly, lists the obstacles to the development of natural literary talent, among them being one he entitles "the Pram in the Hall," which, being interpreted, means domestic cares and responsibilities. Our poet, if the poem is indeed autobiographical, may have been feeling that his artistic talent was vitiated by his having married romantically and too young. An older poem in the bardic metre, *Don Bhothán is Deacair Bóin* (It's hard to support a cabin), is more explicit in expressing the poet's frustration at finding himself having to support what he describes as "a small sharp-tongued unprofitable wife and a brood of sullen brats."

The Poem: Like the author of the previous poem, this poet uses exaggeration for effect, but in this case he is blaming himself as much as anyone else for his troubles. The piece is quite modern, late 19th or early 20th Century, and is more of a droll comic song than a poem. It is set to a popular air to which other songs in Irish and English are sung. For this reason I have kept strictly to the metre of the original, and anyone who can strum three chords on the guitar will find it worth singing in Irish or English.

THE SPINNING WHEEL

A year before marrying the love of my heart
Six whole pounds of flax she'd have spun in a
round,
But as soon as we settled beneath the same
thatch
She took three months to finish the one single
pound.

Chorus:
Och, my wife and my care and my spinning-
wheel fine,
My few pounds of wool left forever unspun,
Two days she must rest for one day up and
dressed –
O sweet God, see me soon from this burden
undone!

When I thought I had chosen a wife of the best,
So mild and so modest, the pick of the lot,
I soon found I was doomed to a life of unrest,
A heart full of malice was all she had got.

When she hears me approaching the house
from the fields
She stokes up the fire with a great pile of turf,
Sets the children to working all head over heels
And sits in to the spinning wheel all in a fuss.

A long life with this wife is a life I don't need,
May she have a short life and be soon a dead
loss,
I'd go tramping the country her brood for to
feed
If three months from today I could shoulder her
box.

Final chorus:

Och, my wife and my care and my spinning-
wheel fine,
My few pounds of wool left forever unspun,
Her baccy to hand and her pipe glowing grand
And what matter the rent-money scattered and
gone!

AN TUIRNÍN LÍN

An bhliain sular phósas-sa stór mo chroí
Ba ghairid mar lón aici sé phunt lín,
Ach ansan nuair a phósas is chuamar i dtíos
Bhíodh bun ag an bpunt aici i gcionn trí mhí.

Curfá:
Och, mo bhean is mo chlann is mo thuirnín lín,
Mo chúpla punt olla go deo gan sníomh,
Dhá lá ina luí in aghaidh lae ina suí –
Is go dtóga Dia dílis a cúram díom!

Nuair a mheasas gur thoghas-sa togha mná tí,
Go tais is go modhúil, ina rogha thar díogha,
Ní hamhlaidh a bhí ach an fala ina croí
Do leag mé im' cheann gan mheabhair gan bhrí.

Nuair a bhraitheann sí mise ag teacht chun an tí
Tine bhreá mhóna a chuireann sí síos,
Stiúraíonn na leanaí ar fud an tí
Is scaoileann ar siúl an tuirnín lín.

Tá bean agam féin is nár mhaire mé í,
Nár mhaire sí agam is nár mhaire me í,
Dá mb'éigean dom Éire a shiúl lena clainn
Go rabhad faoina cróchar i gceann trí mhí.

Curfá:
Och, mo bhean is mo chlann is mo thuirnín lín,
Mo chúpla punt olla go deo gan sníomh,
Tobac ar a bois agus píopa len' ais
'S is cuma sa domhan cá ngabhann an cíos.

The Little White Horse

The Poet: Seoirse Seártan was born in 1879 in Béal Átha an Ghaorthaidh near Macroom in West Cork, one of the small pockets of territory where the Irish language survived into this century as the daily language of the people. A visitor to that village today will get "Céad Míle Fáilte" in the pub which bears the family name. Seoirse received a secondary school education at the famous North Monastery Christian Brothers School in Cork City. He emigrated to Liverpool, but maintained his interest in the Irish language, eventually becoming president of the Liverpool branch of the Gaelic League in the years before the First World War. When he heard from his father the sad news of the demise of the family's beloved if idiosyncratic little mare he sent home this comic elegy, which was later published in the Irish language newspaper, *Fáinne an Lae*. He died in Liverpool in 1957.

The Poem: Like the previous poem, this one is set to a popular air and is still sung. It happens also to be one of my own favourite songs, not just for itself but for the nostalgic reason that I learned it many years ago in that same West Cork area where the Little White Horse lived and died. Under a scholarship scheme operated by the Gaelic League to send children from English-language cities and towns to spend a month of their summer school holidays learning Irish as a living language in some Irish-language area, on a fine summer's day in 1937 I set out with a bus-load of other students – at nine years, I was the "baby" of the group – from my native Limerick to the village of Cúil Aodha which is only down the road from the poet's native village. During our month in the Gaeltacht (the name by which the Irish-languge areas are collectively known) we had a daily class in Irish along with the more welcome experience of rural life as it was then lived, and among the songs I brought back in my head and in my soul was *An Capaillín Bán* which, as was the custom in our family, I subsequently taught to my brothers and sisters.

THE LITTLE WHITE HORSE

Alas and alack! but 'tis Death deals the heavy blow
When it knocks down that friend we would wish
never to go;
Not for men, not for women or boys do I make this
verse
But a poorly-got mare that we called the Little
White Horse.

In well-watered Iveleary 'twas there she lived all
her life,
She never grew much, 'twas her nature from every
side;
Tho' of meal and of oats in sackfuls she made a
short course
It showed little result on the hide of the Little
White Horse.

The Eight Sages' sense was packed into that little
mare's head;
Of music she loved what was sweet and hated the
bad;
Coming home from Macroom if you struck up a
bar of a verse
East or South wind couldn't catch the Little White
Horse.

One eye she had lost, and not likely to find it
again;
With only one left her pleasure and life-style were
plain;
But the eye of the Cyclops or a hovering hawk o'er
the gorse
Were no match for the one in the head of the Little
White Horse.

Her legs were but weak tho' the doctor prescribed
her a bottle,
So crooked and knobby she seldom could move at
full throttle:
I remember a day when only one leg stayed the
course,
Then a raggedy, wobbly mare was that Little White
Horse.

At long last 'twas the will of our Holy Father on
high
To send his grim messenger telling her she had to
die;
That poor mare got an elegant burial: now ending
my verse
I pray solace and peace on the soul of the Little
White Horse.

AN CAPAILLÍN BÁN

Mo chreach is mo chás 'sé an bás a thagann go
trom,
Nuair a leagtar ar lár an cara gur mhaith linn bheith
buan;
Ní le fearaibh, le mnáibh ná le buachaillí
bhaineann mo dhán
Ach le láirín droch-mhianaigh ar a nglaoidís an
Capaillín Bán.

In Uíbh Laoghaire na nGaortha 'sea a chaith sise a
saol.
Níor fhás sí puinn riamh, mar ba dhual di ó gach
taobh dá gaol,
Gidh gur mó mála coirce 'gus mine a d'ith sí go
slán
Is fíor-bheag dá chomhartha bhí ar chraiceann an
Chapaillín Bháin.

Do bhí ciall na n-ocht nduine chliste i gceann an
láirín,
D'aithneodh sí an deifir bhí idir droch-cheol is ceol
binn,
Ag filleadh ó Mhaigh Chromtha abhaile buail suas
amhrán
'S ní bhéarfadh gaoth anoir nó aneas ar an
gCapaillín Bán.

Bhí súil léi imithe gan aon choinne go bhfillfeadh
go deo,
Do bhí sí ar leathshúil gan dúil le sonas ná só,
Ach dá ghéire radharc Cyclops nó an seabhac ar
lorg préacháin
Is suarach ab fhiú iad seachas súilín an Chapaillín
Bháin.

A chosa níor láidir cé gur tháinig buidéal ón
ndochtúir,
Chomh cam cnapánach, gan dásacht, gan
deiseacht, gan lúth;
Is cuimhin liomsa lá ná raibh slán ach an t-aon
chos amháin
Is ba ghiobalach fánach an láir í, an Capaillín Bán.

Fé dheireadh thiar thall dob fhonn le hAthair na
nGrás
A theachtaire dúbhach a chur chuici le scéala an
bháis;
Do cuireadh go g'lánta an láir bhocht: sin deireadh
mo dháin,
Is síocháin 'gus sólás go bhfaighe anam an
Chapaillín Bháin.

Tulyar

The Poet: Seán Ó Ríordáin was born in County Cork in 1917, and like other young writers of the period during and immediately after the Second World War, he was influenced both by the general resurgence of patriotic feeling in that period as well as by the philosophic and cultural views of Daniel Corkery, the writer, artist and scholar who was then Professor of English at the university in Cork. Ó Ríordáin soon gained a reputation as the most original post-war poet in the Irish language – so original, indeed, that some of the older and more pedantic scholars and writers accused him of not writing proper Irish at all! Unfortunately, a bout of tuberculosis, and subsequent continual ill-health, prevented him from fulfilling his early promise, and his output remained small but significant. Like another talented writer, the three-named Brian O'Nolan, Flann O'Brien/Myles na Gopaleen, the poet Ó Ríordáin wasted much of his talent and energy in writing a weekly column for the *Irish Times* – "ad delectationem stultorum" ("to amuse fools") as the scribe of *Táin Bó Cuailgne* puts it (having in the previous sentence wished a blessing on all who would memorize that great story without altering it!).

The Poem: Perhaps because of his ill-health, Ó Ríordáin was more inclined to morbid sarcasm than to any form of humour, even the satiric. The poem is one of his rare exercises in the comic genre; even in this he uses the purchase of a stallion for the newly-created Irish National Stud as a pretext for sardonic comment on the sexual mores of the nation. As a bachelor, he might be accused of counselling others to do what he took care not to do himself; but at least his poor health was an excuse not available to Brian Merriman, the exuberant author of *Cúirt an Mheán Oíche*, who, although he subsequently married, is said to have been a bachelor when he poetically had the young women of Ireland not only accusing the men of making arranged matches with well-off older women, but even urging the well-fed clergy to marry and produce legitimately children like the fine specimens to be found in every parish and whose resemblance to the local priest was remarkable!

TULYAR

O Tulyar, O Stallion,
Bought by De Valera from the Aga Khan,
A most chaste land, my ancestral land,
Land of virgins, land of abbots,
Land of psalters and of gospels
And friars poor but great in learning.
That is history, Tulyar:
But now, Stallion, give ear:
Don't you think it somewhat strange
That a practitioner of your fame

Surpassing every horsey name
To us came
Here to exercise your trade
In land of scholars, land of saints,
Land blest by Patrick when *he* came?
Not that it's sin when horses mate,
But your coming has set seed a-shake;
Not Patrick's gospel do you bring
But quite a different thing
That Eisirt would understand.
Sin is less sinful in our land
Now that you at stud will stand,
A public stallion, with official backing,
On behalf of government acting.
Was it that we had gone all barren
And needed the example of a stallion?
Or were we to be deemed heretical
Unless you were classified official?

TULYAR

A Tulyar, a Stail,
A cheannaigh De Valéra ón Aga Khan,
Tír mhór geanmnaíochta tír mo shean,
Tír maighdean, tír ab,
Tír saltar is soiscéal,
Is bráthar bocht ar mhórán léinn.
A Tulyar, sin stair:
Ach cogar, a Stail:
Nach dóigh leat é bheith ait
Ceardaí ded cheird, ded chlú, ded chleacht,
Ded chumas breise thar gach each,
A theacht
Ag cleachtadh a cheirde anseo inár measc
I dtír na n-ollamh, tír na naomh,
An tír a bheannaigh Pádraig féin?
Ní hé gur peaca cumasc each,
Ach suathadh síl ab ea do theacht;
Ní soiscéal Phádraig thugais leat
Ach intinn eile
'Thuigfeadh Eisirt;
Is lú de pheaca peaca, a Stail,
Tú bheith i mbun taithí inár measc,
Id stail phoiblí, lán-oifigiúil,
Thar ceann an rialtais ag feidhmiú.
  An é go rabhamar fachta seasc,
  Gur theastaigh sampla stail' inár measc?
  Nó an rabhamar dulta eiriciúil
  Mura ndéanfaí tusa oifigiúil?

To An Uncouth Seagull

The Poet: An Aran Islander, Ó Direáin entered the Civil Service in his youth and spent over forty years working in an office in the Department of Education in Dublin. In one of his poems he laments the fact that while the stone walls which protect the little fields of Aran are a monument to his ancestors, his corresponding monument will be the heaps of files gathering dust in a Civil Service office. After difficult early years in which he experienced frustration and neglect, he lived long enough to "win fame in the end". His poems are usually short and taut, imitating the pithy style of the bardic poetry; from the old poetry, too, he took some archaic vocabulary which sometimes made his poems difficult for the reader of modern Irish. Personally he was, in the clichè phrase, a "gentle giant of a man," unassuming and modest about his work, an unusual and unhelpful trait in this media-dominated age when many of the younger versifiers are more like self-promoting publicists and performers than genuine poets. I once accompanied Ó Direáin on a two-hour circuitous walk in the hinterland of a West of Ireland town – we were taking part in a cultural festival and he wanted, he said, to avoid the afternoon bar interlude between events – and I was both entertained and instructed by the depth of his literary erudition and range of reference. While many of his poems are expressive of nostalgic reminiscence for his native Aran or act as an escape valve for his professional frustration, he could also turn to more literary topics such as the philosopher, Berkeley, and the playwright, Seán O'Casey.

The Poem: The poet was prematurely bald, which explains why a direct hit by a Liffeyside seagull caused him to wince all the more! I reminded him one day that when he first published this poem, in a collection entitled *Cloch Choirnéil*, it was printed in juxtaposition with a poem entitled *Réim na bhFaoileán* (The Seagulls' Domain) in which he decribes the seagulls in Aran as gluttonous and raucous scavengers; obviously, the Aran gulls had sent word to their Liffey cousins to watch out for this big bald human on his poetic perambulations along the city quays; so that the present poem might more properly be entitled *Díoltas na bhFaoileán* (The Seagulls' Revenge).

TO AN UNCOUTH SEAGULL

With so many men and women
In Dublin by the Liffey:
What reason had you, villain!
On a poet to drop your gifty?

Keep your mess to yourself,
Voracious thieving bird,
Never again, long as you live,
Soil this poet with your dirt.

My heart is sufficient sore
To notice as days go on
Your squawking brood outnumber
Noble progeny of the swan.

FAOILEÁN DROCHMHÚINTE

Is a liacht fear is bean
In Áth Cliath cois Life:
Tuige duit, a chladhaire!
Féirín a scaoileadh ar fhile?

Coinnigh do phráib agat féin,
A éin an chraois bhradaigh,
Is le do mharthain arís
An file seo ná salaigh.

Leor mar léan liom
Go bhfeicim go seasta
Gur líonmhaire do ál
Ná pór ard na heala.